Just as I Am

The Aftermath of Charles Finney's Conversion Theology

David C. Hacker

Just as I Am:
The Aftermath of Charles
Finney's Conversion Theology

David C. Hacker

Previously published as *The Role of the Conversion Theology of Charles G. Finney in the Theological Drift of Southern Baptists*, 2021

Revised and Expanded Edition 2023

DEDICATION

For the glory of God, who brought me out of darkness into his marvelous light

CONTENTS

PREFACE

This project is the result of several years of study during which I completed my Bachelor's in Theological Studies and Master's in Theology through International Christian College and Seminary (ICCS). Subsequently, I conducted this project as part of my Doctorate of Theology. It has here been revised and expanded for the public. My journey has been long and arduous. I labored under a false sense of being a Christian due to a spurious childhood profession of faith and baptism. After reaching the depths of my depravity and being imprisoned, I slowly realized that I was only truly born again at the age of forty-five. God used the means of grace during this time to lead me to discover that I had only called myself Christian while my life told a different story. This understanding resulted from studying the Bible, and books sent to me by my loving family. My life was the story of one who was at enmity with God and gave hearty approval to those who practiced iniquity (Romans 1 ESV).

I thank God for the fellow believers He placed in my path during my imprisonment who told me about ICCS. God had providentially furnished me with savings that allowed me to pay for these degrees upfront and finish them after my release.

My theological journey has been arduous. Being raised in a typical Southern Baptist church, I had all of the requisite preconceived Arminian notions. Through study, I became one who believes that "Salvation is of the Lord" (Jonah 3:9). Charles H. Spurgeon aptly sums up my current theological views. He writes, "I have my own private opinion that there is no such a thing as preaching Christ and him crucified, unless you preach what now-a-days is called Calvinism. I have my own ideas, and those I always state boldly. It is a nickname to call it Calvinism; Calvinism is the gospel, and nothing else." [1] Similarly, I can wholeheartedly state with George Whitefield: "I embrace the

[1] C. H. Spurgeon, "Christ Crucified," in *The New Park Street Pulpit Sermons*, vol. 1 (London: Passmore & Alabaster, 1855), 50.

calvinistical scheme, not because Calvin, but JESUS CHRIST, I think, has taught it to me."[2]

My interest in this particular topic resulted from my desire to learn more about the origins of my denomination, Southern Baptists. They began as Calvinistic Baptists who believed in the sovereignty of God in salvation. Yet, today, the majority are Arminian Baptists who believe salvation is ultimately determined by man's acceptance or rejection of an offer of salvation. Growing up as a Southern Baptist, I had honestly never even heard of the doctrines of grace. I had always been taught to read and interpret the Bible in a way that upheld man's free will and made him the ultimate factor in whether one would be saved. I was amazed to learn that the Southern Baptist Convention (SBC) had been founded on the belief that God is sovereign in salvation.

I cannot thank God enough for Corey Perkins, former pastor of Oak Grove Baptist Church. He and the godly men there persevered with me through Bible studies on the doctrines of grace. These men have been willing to correct me when I was wrong and explore new ideas that I had not considered before with me. I thank God for putting these men in my life. They are what true Christian fellowship in the body of Christ is about—studying God's word, encouraging one another, and holding one another accountable.

I am also thankful that God providentially guided me to Grace Bible Theological Seminary (GBTS) in Conway, AR, where I am currently pursuing my Master of Divinity degree. The godly men leading and teaching there have given me invaluable insight into research methodology. GBTS provides an atmosphere that cultivates a band of brothers who study God's Word together as they prepare to go out and serve His church.

The work that ICCS does in providing low-cost theological education to the incarcerated so that they can go out into the world and preach the gospel upon their release is invaluable. I want to thank Dr. William McCorkle at ICCS for his willingness to adapt my plan of study to my particular theological interests. This flexibility allowed me to study in areas where I needed to grow the most.

David C. Hacker

Ashdown, Arkansas
August 2023

[2] George Whitefield, "Letter CCCCLVIII," in *The Works of the Reverend George Whitefield*, vol. 1 (London: Edward & Charles Dilly, 1871), 442 (emphasis original).

1

INTRODUCTION

The struggle within the church for doctrinal purity and the fight against doctrinal drift is not new by any means. The debate over God's sovereignty in salvation versus man's free will has been ongoing for the last two thousand years. Thomas Bradwardine's (ca. 1290–1349) work, *The Cause of God Against the Pelagians,* puts into words the feelings many have likely had about this controversy throughout the centuries. He writes,

> As in the times of old four hundred and fifty prophets of Baal strove against a single prophet of God; so now, O Lord, the number of those who strive with Pelagius against thy free grace cannot be counted. They pretend not to receive grace freely, but to buy it. The will of men (they say) should precede, and thine should follow: theirs is the mistress, and thine the servant.... Alas! nearly the whole world is walking in error in the steps of Pelagius. Arise, O Lord, and judge thy cause.[3]

Just as Bradwardine did not resolve these issues in his day, it is unlikely that anyone will settle them in the present day. Those walking in the error of Pelagius have only increased since Charles Grandison Finney resurrected and popularized this age-old heresy. Nevertheless, we as Christians must endeavor to set forth the truth of "our fall in Adam, and the necessity of our new birth in Christ Jesus," as George Whitefield often exclaims in his journals.[4]

In his classic book, *The Holiness of God,* Dr. R. C. Sproul states, "[T]here have been only three generic types of theology competing for acceptance

---

[3] Thomas Bradwardine, *The Cause of God Against the Pelagians*, 1344, quoted in J. H. Merle D'Aubigné, *History of the Reformation in the Sixteenth Century*, trans. Henry Beveridge, vol. 5 (Glasgow: William Collins, 1862), 75.

[4] George Whitefield, *George Whitefield's Journals*, ed. Iain Murray (Edinburgh: Banner of Truth Trust, 1989), 102.

within the Christian Church."[5] He, of course, is referring to Pelagianism,[6] Semi-Pelagianism,[7] and Augustinianism.[8] Liberalism currently embodies Pelagianism. Roman Catholicism and Arminianism are examples of Semi-Pelagianism. Reformed theology, often called Calvinism, represents Augustinianism. As Sproul points out, "Pelagianism is not Christian."[9] Still, Semi-Pelagianism and Augustinianism are both systems debated among believing Christians. Semi-Pelagianism holds to the basic tenants of Christianity and "is the majority report among evangelical Christians, [yet it] still represents a theology of compromise with our natural inclinations."[10] Thus, Semi-Pelagianism is a vast misunderstanding of the sovereignty of God and man's ability to *make decisions* for Christ. Scripture says that one must be born again to see the kingdom of God, which requires the work of the Holy Spirit (John 3:1–8). Just as we had no choice in our natural birth, we have no choice in our being born again. Yet, Arminianism teaches that those who are at enmity with God *choose* to be born again. Scripture is clear that, in our natural state, man is dead in his trespasses and sins (Ephesians 2:1). Sproul concludes, "The failure of modern evangelicalism is the failure to understand the holiness of God. If that one point were grasped, there would be no more talk of mortal enemies of Christ coming to Jesus by their own power."[11]

Arminians and Calvinists can debate and agree to disagree on these issues as fellow Christians and brothers in Christ. However, both should reject those who hold Pelagian views. This book aims to show where Finney, and

---

[5] R. C. Sproul, *The Holiness of God* (Wheaton, IL: Tyndale House, 2013), 182.

[6] "The teachings associated with Pelagius, a British monk who taught in Rome in the late 4th and early 5th centuries AD. Pelagianism taught that people are capable of avoiding sin and choosing to live righteous lives even apart from God's grace. Pelagius rejected the ideas of original sin and predestination. He believed that people were not inherently sinful and that they were able to live holy lives in accordance with God's will and merit salvation by good works." (John D. Barry et al., eds., "Pelagianism," in *The Lexham Bible Dictionary* [Bellingham, WA: Lexham Press, 2016]).

[7] "The Semipelagian view … held that grace was crucial in salvation but that the initial steps toward Christian faith were to be taken by 'free' human will. God would respond, in this view, by offering more grace, and thus a synergistic salvific process would ensue." (Nathan P. Feldmeth, "SemiPelagianism," in *Pocket Dictionary of Church History: Over 300 Terms Clearly and Concisely Defined* [Downers Grove: InterVarsity Press, 2008]).

[8] "Augustinianism … starts with the complete sinfulness of humankind (depravity), which leaves humans unable to respond in faith toward God. In keeping with this, Augustinianism asserts that God predestines those who are enabled to repent and believe." (Stanley Grenz, David Guretzki, and Cherith Fee Nordling, "Augustine, Augustinianism (354–430)," in *Pocket Dictionary of Theological Terms* [Downers Grove: InterVarsity Press, 1999]).

[9] Sproul, *The Holiness of God*, 182.

[10] Sproul, 182.

[11] Sproul, 183.

many of his followers, stand on this spectrum. It will demonstrate how different the current theology of Southern Baptists is from that which their founders held, and Southern Baptists continued to believe for almost a century.[12]

Although not a Baptist himself, Dr. Michael S. Horton stated in March of 1995, "Jerry Falwell called [Finney] 'one of my heroes and a hero to many evangelicals, including Billy Graham. I recall wandering through the Billy Graham Center some years ago, observing the place of honor given to Finney in the evangelical tradition, reinforced by the first class in theology I had at a Christian college, where Finney's work was required reading."[13] Unfortunately, the view of Finney as a hero who deserves a place of honor in the evangelical tradition still represents the thought of many Baptists today. In the foreword to a biography of Finney, Billy Graham stated, "Through this Spirit-filled ministry, uncounted thousands came to know Christ in the nineteenth century, resulting in one of the greatest periods of revival in history."[14] As will be seen, this does not accurately reflect history.

A shift from Calvinism to Arminianism occurred in the years after Finney's death. This book will argue that the conversion theology and revival methodology that Finney promoted was a significant factor in the theological drift of Baptists in the south. First, it will demonstrate that southern Baptists were almost unanimously Calvinistic in their theology and soteriology before the formation of the Southern Baptist Convention (SBC) in 1845 and that they remained so after this until around 1920.[15] Next, it will demonstrate that Finney formulated his *new measures* based on his theology. The popularity he gained due to the perceived success of his methodology and theology led to

---

[12] *cf.* Steven Lemke argues that the majority of Baptists were, in fact, not Calvinists. He states that such a claim cannot be made based on "what a few elite leaders believed;" hence, "it would be merely grasping at tulips to count four-point Calvinists as legitimate Calvinists." (Steve W Lemke, "History or Revisionist History? How Calvinistic Were the Overwhelming Majority of Baptists and Their Confessions in the South until the Twentieth Century?," *Southwestern Journal of Theology* 57, no. 2 [Spring 2015]: 232, https://swbtsv7.s3.amazonaws.com/media/Theology_Journal/57.2/57.2_Lemke.pdf).

[13] Michael S. Horton, "The Legacy of Charles Finney," *Modern Reformation* 4, no. 1 (February 1995): 4, https://modernreformation.org/resource-library/articles/the-legacy-of-charles-finney/.

[14] Billy Graham, foreword to *Charles Grandison Finney and the Birth of Modern Evangelism*, by Lewis A. Drummond (London: Hodder & Stoughton, 1983), 6, quoted in Iain H. Murray, *Revival and Revivalism: The Making and Marring of American Evangelicalism; 1750 – 1858* (Edinburgh: Banner of Truth Trust, 2017), 298.

[15] Nettles's "thesis is that Calvinism, popularly called the doctrines of grace, prevailed in the most influential and enduring arenas of Baptist denominational life until the end of the second decade of the twentieth century." (Thomas J. Nettles, *By His Grace and for His Glory: A Historical, Theological and Practical Study of the Doctrines of Grace in Baptist Life*, Revised and Expanded 20th Anniversary Edition [Cape Coral, FL: Founders, 2006], ix).

a theological shift that continues to affect the church today. Calvinism will be defined as the response in the articles of the Synod of Dort to the Arminian Remonstrants. They can be summarized as God's predestination, the death of Christ and the redemption of humans through that death, the corruption of humans, conversion to God with its way of happening, and the perseverance of the saints.[16] The *1689 London Baptist Confession of Faith* also articulates these doctrines.

Chapter two will survey the historical evidence of the Calvinistic roots of Southern Baptists and give a brief overview of Baptist origins in England, including the founding of the first Baptist church in the colonies in the seventeenth century. Then it will discuss developments in the Baptist doctrine of salvation in the eighteenth and nineteenth centuries. It will conclude with trends that emerged in the twentieth century, focusing specifically on the significant events of the first few decades of that century.

Chapter three will give a brief overview of the traditional, or Calvinistic, Baptist view of conversion that was the majority prior to the mid-nineteenth century. It will provide a short contrast of the two predominant views held by evangelicals, Arminianism and Calvinism. Next, an example will show how uncommon the views of conversion popularized in the mid to late nineteenth century had been previously.

Chapter four will outline Finney's conversion theology and methodology and the opposition from his contemporaries. It will focus on the specific areas where Finney rejected Reformed orthodoxy.

Chapter five will analyze Finney's rejection of the use of the means of grace. It will explore his thoughts on whether revival and conversion are human or divine, consider his departure from the Edwardsean theological tradition he inherited, discuss his Pelagian and semi-Pelagian tendencies, and refute his conflation of backsliders with false professors. Finally, it will review his propagation of error rather than inventing new theology and methodology. These will demonstrate that Finney's theology is Pelagian at heart.

Chapter six will survey the effects of Finney's theology on southern Baptists and evangelicalism as a whole. It analyzes Finney's polemic rewriting of history and its result on subsequent generations, the consequences of revivalism, the specific effects of Finney's theology and methodology on Baptists, and the understanding of God and His role in conversion, as well as his theology's influence on church practice.

---

[16] See W. Robert Godfrey, *Saving the Reformation: The Pastoral Theology of the Canons of Dort* (Orlando, FL: Reformation Trust, 2019); See also Cook, who defines Calvinism as "God's sovereignty, human inability to affect conversion in any way, and divine election." (Matthew W. Cook, "The Impact of Revivalism upon Baptist Faith and Practice in the American South Prior to the Civil War" [PhD diss., Waco, TX, Baylor University, 2009], 20, https://baylor-ir.tdl.org/bitstream/handle/2104/5372/Matthew_Cook_phd.pdf).

The final chapter will summarize the ill effects of Finney's theology and methodology that linger in the church today. This summary is followed by some practical and pastoral applications for the church today and a final warning.

2

HISTORICAL EVIDENCE OF THE CALVINISTIC ROOTS OF SOUTHERN BAPTISTS

The historical roots of southern Baptists trace back through the Particular Baptist movement and Puritanism. Thus they have traditionally upheld a Calvinistic soteriology based on the doctrines of grace.[17] Their views slowly changed in the nineteenth century. These changes continued through the early to mid-twentieth century when Calvinism became the minority view among southern Baptists. R. T. Kendall, in the preface to his 1973 M.A. Thesis, "The Rise And Demise of Calvinism in the Southern Baptist Convention," states:

> I became fascinated with the influence of Calvinism upon Southern Baptists. It took very little investigation to discover that the impact of Calvinism was enormous. Moreover, it did not take long to discover that the Calvinism that exists [in the 1970s] among Southern Baptists is only a remnant of that which originally existed.[18]

This statement is an accurate summary of the historical facts.

Baptists and Calvinism in England

The division of the Baptists between Arminian or General—so-called because they affirmed general atonement—and Calvinistic or Particular—so-

---

[17] Gordon L. Belyea, "Origins of the Particular Baptists," *Themelios* 32, no. 3 (April 2007): 40, http://tgc-documents.s3.amazonaws.com/themelios/Themelios32.3.pdf; Cook also states, "Baptist identity emerged out of its Puritan heritage." (Cook, "The Impact of Revivalism," 28).

[18] Robert Tillman Kendall, "The Rise and Demise of Calvinism in the Southern Baptist Convention" (MA thesis, University of Louisville, 1973), iv, https://www.proquest.com/openview/257efa04cdc28990898524657353276c.

called because they affirmed particular atonement—began in England.[19] The common understanding is that Baptist life grew out of Calvinistic Puritanism and Separatism. Still, some believe that the General Baptists, in particular, were influenced by the Mennonites and Anabaptists and therefore rejected the more prominent features of Calvinism.[20] Gordon L. Belyea, however, believes that the Particular and General Baptists represent two "different movement[s] with separate roots."[21]

The Particular Baptists arose out of a Separatist congregation after adopting believer's baptism in 1638, affirming baptism by immersion in 1641, and producing the *First London Confession* in 1644. This document distinguished the Particular Baptists from the extreme radical revolutionaries (Anabaptists) on the continent while affirming Reformed soteriology.[22] William L. Lumpkin concludes, "Perhaps no Confession of Faith has had so formative an influence on Baptist life as this one."[23] The subsequent *Second London Confession* was intended to identify Baptists with the larger body of non-Anglican Protestants. Thus, it retained most of the *Westminster Confession of Faith's* language while incorporating some changes from the *Savoy Declaration.* It differed only in the distinctives of Baptist belief. Particular Baptists remained faithful to the doctrines of grace until the last half of the nineteenth century.

In contrast, General Baptists were plagued with doctrinal deviation and eventual apostasy, from Socinianism[24] into Unitarianism,[25] from the late eighteenth century.[26] John C. Ryland, a particular Baptist, could say in a

---

19 Much of this overview of Baptist History is indebted to Nettles, *By His Grace.*

20 Ascol records, "Smyth did not remain a Baptist long. He soon joined the Mennonites." (Thomas K. Ascol, *From the Protestant Reformation to the Southern Baptist Convention: What Hath Geneva to Do with Nashville*, Revised edition [Cape Coral, FL: Founders, 2013], 25).

21 Belyea, "Origins of the Particular Baptists," 41, 51.

22 Ascol, *Reformation to the Southern Baptist Convention*, 26–27.

23 William Latane Lumpkin, *Baptist Confessions of Faith* (Valley Forge, PA: Judson, 1959), 152.

24 "Socinianism's unique teachings include the view that the doctrine of the Trinity was neither presented in nor deducible from Scripture. Socinians said the Holy Spirit is nowhere called God in Scripture.... Socinians generally held that a plurality of persons in one divine essence was not possible." (Richard C. Gamble, "Socinianism," in *Encyclopedia of the Reformed Faith*, ed. Donald K. McKim [Louisville: Westminster John Knox, 1992]).

25 "[T]he radical form of Christian belief which rejects the doctrine of the Trinity and the unique divinity of Jesus Christ and affirms uncompromisingly the unity of God." (Arthur J. Long, "Unitarianism," in *The Dictionary of Historical Theology*, ed. Trevor A. Hart [Carlisle, Cumbria, U.K.: Paternoster, 2000]).

26 Nettles, *By His Grace*, 4, 21; See Spilsbery who lists these deviations as rejection of original sin, the affirmation of free will, the assertion of universal atonement, and the affirmation

Circular Letter of the Northamptonshire Baptist Association in 1777, "At present, blessed be God we believe there is no apparent apostasy in our ministers and people from the glorious principles we profess."[27] The letter begins with a concise statement of these "glorious principles" that they held as an association:

> Maintaining the important Doctrines of Three Persons in the Godhead, Eternal and Personal Election; Original Sin; Particular redemption; Free Justification by the imputed Righteousness of Christ; Efficacious Grace in Regeneration; The Final Perseverance of the Saints; and the independency, or Congregational; Order of the Churches of Christ inviolably.[28]

By 1864 changes were already beginning. That year the chairman of the Baptist Union stated that the aim of the churches should be "the supercession on practicable, sound and safe principles of the distinction between General and particular Baptists." [29] Yet, no official action was taken at that time. An official union between General and Particular Baptists did not occur until 1891. This controversy caused Charles Haddon Spurgeon to secede from the Baptist Union in 1887.[30]

Baptists and Calvinism in the United States

In the "Historical Introduction" to *Annals of the American Pulpit: Volume VI (Baptist),* which covers the period from the early settlement of America until 1855, William B. Sprague states that "The prevailing Theology of the Baptists is Calvinism—generally of the type of Andrew Fuller, but occasionally rising to that of Dr. Gill."[31]

---

that one may fall away from grace. (John Spilsbery, *A Treatise Concerning the Lawfull Subject of Baptism*, Second Edition Corrected and Enlarged [London: Henry Hills, 1652], 74).

[27] John C. Ryland, *The Beauty of Social Religion, or, the Nature and Glory of a Gospel Church, Represented in a Circular Letter*, Northamptonshire Baptist Association (Northampton: T. Dicey, 1777), 7.

[28] Ryland, 1.

[29] Ernest A. Payne, *The Baptist Union* (London: Carey Kingsgate, 1959), 26, quoted in Nettles, *By His Grace*, xxx.

[30] Thomas J. Nettles, *Living by Revealed Truth: The Life and Pastoral Theology of Charles Haddon Spurgeon* (Fearn, Ross-Shire: Mentor, 2015), 228.

[31] William B. Sprague, *Annals of the American Pulpit, or, Commemorative Notices of Distinguished American Clergymen of Various Denominations: From the Early Settlement of the Country to the Close of the Year Eighteen Hundred and Fifty-Five: With Historical Introductions*, vol. VI (New York: R. Carter, 1860), xvi.

Seventeenth Century Roots

When Roger Williams immigrated to the New World, he brought the Calvinism of his separatist Puritanism. In 1639 he founded the Baptist Church of Providence, Rhode Island. Under Williams's influence, John Clarke became a Baptist. He founded Newport's second Baptist church in America, which "maintained the doctrine of efficacious grace."[32] The church had adopted immersion as the proper mode of baptism by 1644.[33] In writing about John Clarke and the Baptist church in Newport, Rev. John Callender states, "He left behind him a statement, in manuscript. Of his religious opinions, from which it appears that, with the distinctive views of the Baptists he united those which are commonly called Calvinistic."[34] Likewise, the First Baptist Church in Boston was also Calvinistic from its inception.

Into the Eighteenth and Nineteenth Centuries

Benjamin Keach's son, Elias, arrived in the New World as an unconverted man. He soon came under conviction and was converted as he preached one of his father's sermons. Subsequently, he was instrumental in founding the first Baptist church in Pennsylvania, in Philadelphia. The five Baptist churches in Philadelphia in 1707 formed the Philadelphia Baptist Association, the first in America. The association based its confession of faith on the *Second London Baptist Confession,* a thoroughly Calvinistic document.

In his biographical sketch of *The Callenders,* Sprague makes an interesting observation about the calling and ordination of Jeremy Condy as pastor of First Baptist Church, Boston, in 1739:

> In his doctrinal views *he was reputed to be an Arminian;* and, after about four years, a number of his members became so much dissatisfied with him on this account that they withdrew and formed the Second Baptist Church.... He was a man of unblemished character, though the church *does not appear to have prospered greatly* under his ministry.[35]

This sketch demonstrates not only that Calvinism was the predominant doctrine of Baptists then but also the effects that Arminianism can have on church growth. Nettles states, "So strong was the Calvinism of this

---

[32] Thomas Armitage, *A History of the Baptists: Traced by Their Vital Principles and Practices, from the Time of Our Lord and Saviour Jesus Christ to the Present,* Revised and Enlarged Edition (New York: Bryan, Taylor, 1890), 671.

[33] Ascol, *Reformation to the Southern Baptist Convention*, 29.

[34] Sprague, *Annals of the American Pulpit,* VI:25.

[35] Sprague, VI:37n* (emphasis added).

association that in 1752 it passed a resolution affirming that such as rejected the doctrine of unconditional election could not be members of the churches."[36]

While the General Baptists fared better in the northern colonies, the Particular Baptists took the lead in the middle and southern colonies.[37] The first Baptist church in the south was Calvinistic in its doctrine. Sprague notes, "William Screven … was instrumental [in] gathering the First Baptist Church in Charleston, S.C., and became its Pastor."[38] Matthew Cook, writing about this initial congregation at Charleston, states, "What the available information indicates is that despite the fact that an earlier generation of Baptists had parted company with official Puritanism in New England, the faith and practice of these early southern Baptists still showed them to be largely in keeping with a Puritan heritage."[39] He indicates that this heritage included adopting the "London Confession" in 1700, which was "highly Calvinistic in nature."[40]

Cook concludes that "there is sufficient evidence to indicate that the Charleston church placed a high value on theological correctness (from a Calvinistic perspective) throughout Screven's tenure."[41] In the funeral sermon for the church's next pastor, Oliver Hart, it was said, "In his religious principles he was a fixed Calvinist, and a consistent … Baptist. The doctrines of *free efficacious grace* were precious to him."[42] Cook states, "Hart kept a careful record of his preaching during his ministerial tenure. An examination of that record shows Hart's fondness for doctrinal content with a Calvinistic bent. Other than the gospels, Hart (sic) most frequent choice of texts was from the book of Romans, with its emphasis upon human sinfulness and inability."[43] In 1751, when Hart founded the Charleston Association, its doctrinal understanding came from the *Second London Baptist Confession*.[44] One should

---

[36] Nettles, *By His Grace*, xxxviii.

[37] Ascol, *Reformation to the Southern Baptist Convention*, 29.

[38] Sprague, *Annals of the American Pulpit*, VI:34n†.

[39] Cook, "The Impact of Revivalism," 35.

[40] Cook, 43.

[41] Cook, 43.

[42] Sprague, *Annals of the American Pulpit*, VI:49 (emphasis original).

[43] Cook, "The Impact of Revivalism," 62.

[44] The *Philadelphia Confession of Faith* (1742) added an article on the laying on of hands and also one on the singing of psalms, hymns, and spiritual songs to the *Second London Baptist Confession*. The 1767 *Charleston Confession* was based on the *Philadelphia Confession* but omitted the article on the laying on of hands." (Michael A.G. Haykin, foreword to *Confessing the Faith: The 1689 Baptist Confession for the 21st Century* [Cape Coral, FL: Founders Press, 2012], 5, 5n1).

not underestimate the influence of the Charleston Association in establishing Reformation theology in the Baptist movement of the South.[45]

An aggressive and warm Calvinism swallowed up the few General Baptist congregations in the south during the First Great Awakening. The Sandy Creek Association, the most influential Separatist Baptist grouping of the eighteenth century, adopted a soteriologically Calvinistic confession. One should note that many of these Separate Baptist churches were originally Congregationalists, which held to the *Savoy Declaration,* a Reformed confession of faith. They had become convinced of believers' baptism during the Great Awakening and subsequently became Baptists.[46] Likewise, when Separate Baptists and Regular Baptists united in Virginia, their doctrinal basis was the *Philadelphia Confession of Faith.*

In the late 1700s, John Witherspoon could affirm, "The [B]aptists are [P]resbyterians in all other respects, only differing in the point of infant baptism."[47] By this statement, he meant that both denominations held to a Calvinistic confession of faith. Francis Asbury was the co-founder of the Methodist Episcopal Church in America. He wrote in a personal letter to John Wesley on September 20, 1783: "Maryland does not abound with Calvinism; but in Virginia, North and South Carolina, and Georgia, the Baptists labor to stand by what they think is the good old cause."[48] He recommends that Wesley "always keep the front of the Arminian Magazine filled with the best pieces … against Calvinism."[49] This statement is evidence that Calvinism was the majority theology among Baptists in these areas where the Methodists were working.

The tendency for theological drift is ever-present. Isaac Backus, near the end of his life in 1797, wrote:

> The enmity which men have discovered against the sovereignty of the grace of God, as revealed in Holy Scriptures, hath now prevailed so far, that every art is

---

[45] Ascol, *Reformation to the Southern Baptist Convention,* 32; *cf.* Lemke asserts that "some Baptist leaders, particularly the children of the wealthy aristocracy of the South, many of whom were educated at elite Ivy League type schools" were Calvinistic in their theology, but they do not represent the "overwhelming majority of Southern Baptists." (Lemke, "History or Revisionist History?," 228) However, he fails to conclusively prove his case.

[46] Ascol, *Reformation to the Southern Baptist Convention,* 32, 38; Based on a false dichotomy of what constitutes *Calvinism,* Lemke claims that those in the Sandy Creek tradition were not overwhelmingly Calvinistic in their soteriology. (Lemke, "History or Revisionist History?," 233).

[47] John Witherspoon, *The Works of the Rev. John Witherspoon* (Philadelphia: William W. Woodward, 1801), 306.

[48] Francis Asbury, *The Journal and Letters of Francis Asbury,* ed. J. Manning Potts, vol. III (London: Epworth, 1958), 30.

[49] Asbury, III:30–31.

> made use of to put other senses upon the words of revelation than God intended therein. He said to Moses: "I will have mercy on whom I will have mercy, and I will have compassion, on whom I will have compassion. So then it is not of him that willeth, nor of him that runneth, but of God that showeth mercy, Ro. 9: 15, 16. This was the doctrine which God made use of in all the reformation, that was wrought in Germany, England, and Scotland, after the year 1517; and by the same doctrine he wrought all the reformation that has been in our day, both in Europe and America.[50]

By God's grace, it would be some time before these views against the sovereignty of God would become the majority, as will be seen.

Robert B. Semple wrote about the decrease of Baptists and the rise of Methodists in the early nineteenth century. He probingly asks, "Does it arise from the Arminian doctrine being more palatable to the self-righteous heart of man?"[51] This question is precisely the right one to ask because the doctrine of man's depravity and moral inability has always been "folly" to the natural man (2 Corinthians 2:14).

Speaking of Baptists in the south at the turn of the nineteenth century, Cook states:

> Prior to this period, other aspects of Baptist identity were more influential in shaping southern Baptists' theological and methodological identity. Calvinism was a dominant influence in southern Baptist life for most of the eighteenth century.... The earliest southern Baptists inherited, and then maintained a Calvinistic primitivism as a dominant aspect of southern Baptist life well into the nineteenth century.... Conversion remained, just as it had with the ... Puritans something God initiated and an individual human received with no one in between.... Revivalism changed that.... Southern Baptists began minimizing those aspects of Baptist faith and practice which were not immediately applicable in a more conversion-oriented context.... From the 1830s onward, Baptists did generally become less Calvinistic and more Arminian. There are numerous examples of Baptist associational bodies adapting their confessions of faith to make them less explicitly Calvinistic, as well as an even more widespread utilization of "worked up" revivals that used "means" to secure conversions.... For southern Baptists, growth became almost as essential to their identity as what they believed about God, and how they put those beliefs into practice.[52]

Likewise, Leon McBeth states, "A comparison of confessions adopted in 1816 and 1845 by the Sandy Creek Association indicates that in time their

---

[50] Alvah Hovey, *A Memoir of the Life and Times of the Rev. Isaac Backus, A.M.* (Boston: Gould & Lincoln, 1859), 356.

[51] Robert Baylor Semple, *A History of the Rise and Progress of the Baptists in Virginia* (Richmond: Published by the Author, John O'Lynch, Printer, 1810), 296.

[52] Cook, "The Impact of Revivalism," 4, 11, 208, 6, 9, 14.

evangelistic *practices* tended to determine their theology rather than their *theology* guiding their practices."[53]

In 1851 The Southern Baptist Publication Society published P. H. Mell's *Predestination and the Saints' Perseverance,* meant to be a "concise and popular exposition of those doctrines [of Grace] … to counteract the tendencies … to Arminianism."[54] His biography includes an account by a long-time member of the church he pastored in Georgia, Mrs. D. B. Fitzgerald, who states that for Dr. Mell:

> If it was a *Baptist* church it must have doctrines peculiar to that denomination preached to it. And with boldness, clearness and vigor of speech that marked him, he preached to them the doctrines of predestination, election, free-grace, etc. He said it was always *his* business to preach the truth as he found it in God's Word, and leave the matter there, feeling that God would take care of the results.[55]

Similarly, The Southern Baptist Publication Society published John L. Dagg's *Manual of Theology* in 1859. Dagg was the first Southern Baptist theologian to produce a systematic theology. In Book seven, he discusses the "election of grace" given to some and not others, the "natural tendency of human depravity," and the need for "renewing grace." He concludes that we are "compelled to refer the matter to the sovereignty of God."[56] Far from being a "minority report," as some claim, it is evident that experiential Calvinism was the norm in southern Baptist churches in the mid-nineteenth century.[57]

The *New Hampshire Confession of Faith,* produced in 1833, was a reworking of the association's statement of faith to emphasize their rejection of free-will theology that was on the rise among the Free Will Baptists in New Hampshire. It was the same in content as the *Philadelphia* and *Second London* confessions, though briefer. Nettles summarizes the association's position as follows:

---

[53] H. Leon McBeth, *The Baptist Heritage* (Nashville: Broadman & Holman, 1987), 229 (emphasis original).

[54] Patrick Hues Mell, *Predestination and the Saints' Perseverance: Stated and Defended from the Objections of Arminians, in a Review of Two Sermons* (Charleston, SC: Southern Baptist Publication Society, 1851), iv.

[55] P. H. Mell Jr., *Life of Patrick Hues Mell* (Louisville: Baptist Book Concern, 1895), 59 (emphasis original).

[56] J. L. Dagg, *Manual of Theology, First Part: A Treatise on Christian Doctrine* (Charleston, SC: Southern Baptist Publication Society, 1859), 313–14.

[57] Lemke, "History or Revisionist History?," 244.

> Rather than interpreting the New Hampshire Confession as a gradual retreat from the Calvinism of former days, it is better to see it as an affirmation of the Calvinistic position on the particular issues raised by the presence and growth of Free Will Baptists in New England. Calvinists did not jettison their distinguishing tenets but rather were saying, "We have a defensible and biblical understanding of the relation of man's will and duty to the doctrines of God's sovereignty."[58]

A cursory review of volume six of Sprague's *Annals* shows that Calvinism was the doctrinal commitment of many of the best-known Baptist pastors. Sprague states that John Gano (1727–1804) embraced the doctrines "contained in the Baptist Confession of Faith, and are commonly styled Calvinistic."[59] He describes Lewis Richards (1752–1832) as "decidedly Calvinistic, without, however, the least approach to Antinomianism."[60] Ambrose Dudley (1750–1823) is said to have been "a thorough Calvinist."[61] Andrew Marshall (1755–1856), the eminent black preacher and pastor of First African Baptist Church in Savannah, GA, from 1806–1856, was said to be "of the old Calvinistic order."[62] Abel Woods(1765–1850) regarded it as "a wonder of free and sovereign grace that a sinner like him should be saved."[63] Benjamin Foster (1750–1798) is said to have been "strictly Calvinistick (sic), and full on the doctrine of salvation by free grace."[64] One could cite numerous other instances, but the evidence is beyond dispute.

David Benedict, writing about the second decade of the nineteenth century, remarks on the distinctive Calvinism among the Baptists before the introduction of a modified Calvinism promoted by advocates of Andrew Fuller:

---

58 Nettles, *By His Grace*, 47; *cf.* Cook, in contrast to Nettles, believes "Baptists in the South did water down their Calvinism.... In the 1840s, multiple southern Baptist associations adopted the New Hampshire Confession of Faith, which omitted several Calvinist doctrines including the notion of a limited atonement." While the specific language of limited atonement is not present in the confession, it seems best to agree with Nettles that Limited Atonement was uncontested among the framers, and that they were attempting to address the pressing issues of free-will theology, in particular. (Cook, "The Impact of Revivalism," 9); Lemke also sees the New Hampshire confession as a rejection of "Limited Atonement," thus he sees the adoption of it as a rejection of Calvinism; however, his definition of *Calvinism* is very limited. (Lemke, "History or Revisionist History?," 244n25).

59 Sprague, *Annals of the American Pulpit*, VI:66.

60 Sprague, VI:202.

61 Sprague, VI:204.

62 Sprague, VI:259.

63 Sprague, VI:316.

64 David Benedict, *A General History of the Baptist Denomination in America: And Other Parts of the World*, vol. 2 (Boston: Manning & Loring, 1813), 304.

> Our old Baptist divines … were generally strong Calvinists as to their doctrinal creed, and but few of them felt at liberty to call upon sinners in plain terms to repent and believe the gospel, on account of their inability to do so without divine assistance. They could preach the gospel before the unconverted, but rousing appeals to their conscience did not constitute a part of their public addresses.… In that age it was customary for many of our ministers to dwell much on the decrees and purposes of God, to dive deep, in their way, into the plans of Jehovah, in eternity, and to bring to light, as they supposed, the hidden treasures of the gospel, which they, in an especial manner, were set to defend.… This extreme of orthodoxy has been followed by laxity and indifference. The Philadelphia Confession of Faith … was the standard of most of the oldest Baptist churches in this country, especially in the middle and southern States … The old Baptists in New England, although, for the most part, they held with their brethren elsewhere the doctrines of Depravity, Election, Divine Sovereignty, Final Perseverance, etc. yet they were not in the habit of enforcing them so strongly as were those in New York, Philadelphia, and further South.… The kind of preaching now much in vogue [in 1860], at the period and among the people [in 1820], would have been considered the quintessence of Arminianism, mere milk and water, instead of the strong meat of the gospel. Then, and with our orthodox Baptists, a sermon would have been accounted altogether defective which did not touch upon Election, Total Depravity, Final Perseverance, etc.… In my early day the Associated Baptists were all professedly Calvinistic in their doctrinal sentiments.… I was not a little surprised at the bitterness of feeling which, in many cases, was displayed by the anti-Calvinists against the doctrine of Election, and of their readiness, in season and out of season, to assail by reason and ridicule. Many could hardly be civil towards their opponents.… Some of [the Methodist] circuit riders of that age conducted as if they considered themselves predestinated to preach against Predestination. And some of our illiterate elders were about a match for them against the Wesleyan creed. And the cry of fatalism on the one hand, and of salvation by works on the other, was continually sounded by the parties.… On the introduction of the Fuller system a very important change followed on the part of many of our ministers in their mode of addressing their unconverted hearers on the subjects of repentance and believing the gospel. Hitherto they would use circumlocution in their discourses on these matters, instead of direct appeals and exhortations to those whose conversion they desired. They would describe the lost condition of sinners and point out the duty of all men to repent and believe the gospel; but beyond this, their views of consistency with the doctrine which ascribes the whole work of salvation to God alone, would not permit them to go.[65]

This account makes it evident that Baptists were beginning to emphasize human instrumentality in the work of conversion in a way not done in the past. These Baptists determined that if man can bring about revival, then man

[65] David Benedict, *Fifty Years Among the Baptists* (1860; repr., Paris, AR: Baptist Standard Bearer, 2001), 136–41.

must be able to respond to the offer of salvation as well. It was but the logical conclusion of this line of thought.

The last half of the nineteenth century saw a gradual decline of Calvinism in the North. Of this decline, Murray states,

> The ultimate success of the new views of evangelism and revival owed much to the loss, sometimes even the suppression, of earlier history. Among the Baptists, as with other denominations, the impressiveness of the claims for the new depended in no small part on an acceptance of the charge that the preceding eras has been largely a story of hyper-Calvinistic barrenness. So effective was the propaganda in most Baptist churches that by the twentieth century their real history was almost entirely unknown.[66]

However, the change was gradual. As late as 1866, *The Baptist Catechism,* based on Benjamin Keach's Catechism of 1640, was issued by the American Baptist Publication Society. Nettles describes it as "clear, forceful, and evangelistic Calvinism."[67] The northern Baptists separated from their Southern counterparts who formed the SBC in 1845. Kendall indicates that, at the SBC's formation, "the theological position of its leaders … —Calvinism— … was taken for granted [as] an assumed presupposition."[68] J. P. Boyce, president of the first Southern Baptist seminary, wrote *A Brief Catechism of Bible Doctrine,* published by the Sunday School Board of the SBC in 1864. The publication notice stated that it "brings out the 'doctrines of grace' and the views of Baptists."[69]

Timothy George notes that all churches that sent delegates to the inaugural meeting that established the SBC had adopted Calvinistic confessions (the *Philadelphia* or *Charleston Confession of Faith* When James P. Boyce was considering a suitable confession for the newly formed Southern Baptist Theological Seminary, he considered the *Philadelphia/Charleston Confession* as the basis. Ultimately, he opted for a more concise statement and commissioned Basil Manly, Jr. to draft the *Abstract of Principle*s based on these confessions.[70]

---

66 Murray, *Revival and Revivalism*, 301. See the section "Conflation of Calvinism and Hyper-Calvinism" in chapter 6 for a further discussion of this topic.

67 Thomas J. Nettles and Steve Weaver, *Teaching Truth, Training Hearts: The Study of Catechisms in Baptist Life*, Revised edition (Cape Coral, FL: Founders, 2017), 19.

68 Kendall, "Rise and Demise of Calvinism," 1.

69 Nettles and Weaver, *Teaching Truth, Training Hearts*, 231.

70 Timothy George, *Baptist Confessions, Covenants, and Catechisms* (Nashville: Broadman & Holman, 1996), 11; *cf.* Lemke claims that the *Philadelphia Confession* was "roundly ignored by the overwhelming number of Southern Baptists after the mid-1800s," and that the authors of the *Abstract of Principles* were aware of these other confessions, but deliberately choose to

Twentieth-century Trends

B. H. Carroll was the founder and first President of Southwestern Baptist Seminary. His life spanned the close of the nineteenth and early part of the twentieth century. Nettles says, "Carroll, intensely concerned that Southwestern Seminary be founded on the 'rocks of predestination,' adhered clearly and strongly to traditional Baptist Calvinism."[71] The foreword to the new and complete edition of Carroll's *An Interpretation of the English Bible* surmises, "These volumes are valuable because of the undisputed position of the author in the minds and hearts of our Baptist people."[72] In his commentary on 1 Peter, one sees a clear display of Carroll's foundation on the doctrines of grace. He writes, "[E]lection was not based upon any foreseen goodness in man or any foreseen repentance or faith in man, but ... repentance and faith proceed from election, and not election from them."[73] These foundational beliefs were still predominant among Southern Baptists as late as 1947.

By the first decade of the twentieth century, there was little difference between the Free Will Baptists and the Northern Baptists, confessionally. The two subsequently merged in 1911. Meanwhile, the formation of the SBC occurred in 1845. It had an unfettered desire for worldwide missions due to its Calvinistic theology. It continued to publish books and sermons defending the doctrines of total depravity, unconditional election, certain and effectual atonement, effectual calling, and perseverance of the saints. The presidents of the SBC for the first fifty years of its existence, the first educators in its seminaries, and its first writing theologians were all distinctively Calvinistic. Nettles states,

---

not use them. (Lemke, "History or Revisionist History?," 249) However, he provides no basis for this claim.

[71] Nettles, *By His Grace*, 176; *cf.* Lemke states, "Carroll might best be described as being in that Calminian perspective of holding in an unresolved tension both Calvinistic views of depravity and election with Arminianistic views of human freedom and responsibility." (Lemke, "History or Revisionist History?," 251n46) However, there is no unresolved *Calminian* tension in Carroll's thought and writing. He, like all Calvinists, affirms both man's depravity and man's responsibility to respond to God's command to repent. This is resolved by the fact that Calvinists acknowledge that man's moral inability, due to depravity, is not a physical inability, rather they do not desire to respond because they are at enmity with God.

[72] John L. Hill, foreword to *The Pastoral Epistles of Paul, 1 and 2 Peter, Jude, and 1, 2, and 3 John*, by B. H. Carroll, ed. J. B. Cranfill, New and Complete Edition, vol. XVI, An Interpretation of the English Bible (Nashville: Broadman, 1947), v.

[73] B. H. Carroll, *The Pastoral Epistles of Paul, 1 and 2 Peter, Jude, and 1, 2, and 3 John*, ed. J. B. Cranfill, New and Complete Edition, vol. XVI, An Interpretation of the English Bible (Nashville: Broadman, 1947), 189.

> The men responsible for the birthing of the Southern Baptist Convention rocked it in the cradle of evangelical, experiential Calvinism.... Southern Baptists were committed to a view of theology that saw God as both Righteous Judge and Sovereign Redeemer and saw man as a rebellious, culpable sinner, helplessly enmeshed in trespasses and sins and in absolute need of sovereign mercy to deliver him.... The first seminary in Southern Baptist life rested on a Calvinistic foundation. In fact, Southern Baptist Theological Seminary, in the eyes of its founders, constituted a bulwark against the gradual encroachments of the Arminian fox into the Southern Baptist vineyard. The seminary's four faculty members, [J. P.] Boyce, [John A.] Broadus, [Basil] Manly, Jr., and [William] Williams, as well as its most ardent promoter, Basil Manly, Sr., shared a common and aggressive commitment to the Doctrines of Grace.[74]

The doctrines of grace were the consensus among Southern Baptists through the second decade of the twentieth century. In 1905 F. H. Kerfoot could still say,

> In common with a large body of evangelical Christians, nearly all Baptists believe what are usually termed the "doctrines of grace," the absolute sovereignty and foreknowledge of God; his eternal and unchangeable purposes or decrees; that salvation in its beginning, continuance and completion, is God's free gift; that, in Christ, we are elected or chosen, personally or individually, from eternity, saved and called out from the world, not according to our works, but according to His own purpose and grace, through the sanctification of the Spirit and belief of the truth; that we are kept by His power from falling away, and will be presented faultless before the presence of His glory."[75]

Similarly, as late as 1955, W. A. Criswell would state, preaching on Isaiah 46:9–11, "That's our God! Now that's what you call foreordination. That's what you call predestination! That's Calvinism! And I am a Calvinist. That's good old Bible doctrine, and I believe the Bible! These things are in God's hands, and ultimately, finally, He purposed it and executeth all of it!"[76]

---

[74] Nettles, *By His Grace*, 108, 136; *cf.* Lemke claims that Southern Baptist Theological Seminary's *Abstract of Principles* "can be claimed to be Calvinistic only by comparison with majoritarian Baptist confessions over the last century-and-a-half which lean even further away from five-point Calvinism." (Lemke, "History or Revisionist History?," 248).

[75] F. H. Kerfoot, "What We Believe According to the Scriptures," in *The Doctrines of Our Faith: A Convenient Handbook for Use in Normal Classes, Sacred Literature Courses and Individual Study*, by Edwin Charles Dargan (Nashville: Sunday School Board, 1905), 230–31.

[76] W. A. Criswell, "Doctrine of Predestination" (Sermon, First Baptist Church of Dallas, November 20, 1955), https://wacriswell.com/sermons/1955/doctrine-of-predestination/; See also W. A. Criswell, "The Effectual Calling of God" (Sermon, First Baptist Church of Dallas, June 5, 1983), https://wacriswell.com/sermons/1983/the-effectual-calling-of-god/ in which Criswell was still promulgating the doctrines of grace in 1983.

The theological drift was slow, and there were shining lights along the way. Nettles describes one of the reasons for the gradual decline into Arminianism in the twentieth century as follows:

> With ever-increasing rapidity, however, concerns focused more and more on denominational programs that minimized and streamlined doctrinal materials. The doctrines were first ignored till they passed from the scene—and finally were either opposed openly as destructive of true piety and mission zeal or discussed as some idiosyncrasy of the past, to be recoiled from with great horror.[77]

The position of many southern Baptists today, claims Nettles, "relegates the sound orthodox years of 1845–1920 to a merely tolerable phase of Southern Baptist thought and treats it with a dismissive spirit."[78]

One can only conclude that subsequent crises over biblical authority, the nature of the atonement, and the uniqueness of Christianity as the way to God directly result from this theological drift. The doctrines of God's sovereignty were abandoned in favor of man's ability.

---

[77] Nettles, *By His Grace*, xlvi.

[78] Thomas J. Nettles, afterword to *"Traditional" Theology & the SBC: An Interaction with, and Response to, The Traditional Statement of God's Plan of Salvation*, Revised Edition (Cape Coral, FL: Founders, 2018), 91.

3

THE CONVERSION THEOLOGY OF BAPTISTS BEFORE FINNEY

As has been seen, the *doctrines of grace* were the hallmark of the biblical soteriology of southern Baptists prior to the influence of revivalism and the resurgence of Semi-Pelagianism/Arminianism. This chapter will briefly overview the distinctives and prevalence of the Calvinistic conversion theology of Baptists in the south before the mid-nineteenth century to set the stage for contrast with Finney's theology and methodology.

Iain Murray contrasts the two views of salvation held by evangelicals, Arminian and Calvinistic, as follows:

> Both Calvinistic and Arminian schools of belief held to the message of salvation as the gift of God through Christ crucified, and both taught the necessity of rebirth, faith, and holiness of life. Disagreement entered over the interpretation of these biblical truths. Evangelical Arminians claimed that grace extends to all men and its acceptance or rejection must therefore depend ultimately on human decision. Calvinists believed that such is the ruined state of human nature that no man would respond to the gospel if repentance and faith are conditions to be fulfilled before grace renews him. They saw repentance and faith, rather, as *parts* of the salvation which God bestows.... Calvinists believed the Scriptures to teach that, in a sovereignty unaccountable to us, those who actually receive Christ are those for whom God intended salvation from all eternity. And further, they believed, that the work of Christ is so definite and particular that he *will save* all those for whom he died. Arminians held that such an understanding of the gospel must obstruct evangelism because it would prevent a preacher telling his hearers that they were able to exercise faith at any time. Calvinists responded that their hope of success in preaching salvation to sinners did not depend in any degree on what they thought man was able to do.[79]

---

[79] Murray, *Revival and Revivalism*, 178–79 (emphasis original).

Murray demonstrates that the ministers experiencing true revival knew they had to deal wisely with those under conviction.[80] Ebenezer Porter (1772–1834) gives an example from his childhood of just how unknown it was in his day that one would call for an immediate decision or assume immediate conversion:

> During a powerful work of grace, which prevailed in my childhood, a zealous preacher, at the close of a public lecture, called on all impenitent sinners, "who would then make up their minds to be on the Lord's side," to rise and declare that purpose by speaking aloud. Scores of hearts in the assembly were ready to burst with deep anxiety, but *the incongruity of such a proposal, in the regular worship of God, was instinctively and generally felt.* After a dead silence of a few moments, five or six men rose, and made the declaration which was desired. I was old enough to observe them all as they spoke, but *among the blessed fruits of that work not one of these was numbered,* and some of them soon became open infidels. But one other instance like this occurred within my knowledge till I became a preacher myself, and not one in all the revivals during my pastoral life.[81]

Murray notes, "These pastors believed that to persuade the convicted to engage in an external act as an aid to conversion, if not as an act of conversion itself was to ignore the magnitude of the spiritual change that brings men from death to life."[82] Thus, one can see that at the beginning of the nineteenth century, the idea of calling for a decision and identifying persons as immediately converted was virtually unknown.

The Calvinistic, or biblical, view of conversion is that "unless one is born again he cannot see the kingdom of God" (John 3:3). Conversion is not a mere moral transformation or making one *nice*. The gospel says, "You must be born again" (v. 7).

The only way into the kingdom of God is to be regenerated by the Holy Spirit (1 Peter 1:3), which recreates one into a new man (2 Corinthians 5:17, Galatians 6:15) and transforms him by giving him a new nature (Colossians 3:10).[83] Conversion is a work of God by faith alone which does not require any specific action on the part of the one that God chooses to show mercy on, such as praying a prayer, walking an aisle, or raising one's hand while all eyes are closed. The Bible emphasizes that God's free grace grants the gift of salvation because He chose to love a wretched sinner in the past for His glory alone. The biblical emphasis is not on how sincere one is but on the fact that

---

[80] Murray, 213.

[81] Ebenezer Porter, *Letters on the Religious Revivals Which Prevailed about the Beginning of the Present Century* (Boston: Congregational Board, 1858), 89–90 (emphasis added).

[82] Murray, *Revival and Revivalism*, 214.

[83] Michael Lawrence, *Conversion: How God Creates a People*, 9Marks: Building Healthy Churches (Wheaton, IL: Crossway, 2017), 23.

one has been saved from God's wrath by no merit of their own. True conversion will lead to a life striving for holiness, even though Christians will often fail and will never be perfect on this side of eternity.

The Calvinistic Conversion Theology of Nineteenth-Century Southern Baptist Theologians

Dagg's 1859 *Manual of Theology*, the first of its kind by a Southern Baptist, devotes an entire section to "Sovereignty of Grace." In it, he covers the major points of Calvinistic, or Reformed, soteriology. He defines the doctrines as follows: Election—"All who will finally be saved, were chosen to salvation by God the Father, before the foundation of the world, and given to Jesus Christ in the covenant of grace." Particular Redemption—"The Son of God gave his life to redeem those who were given to him by the Father in the covenant of grace." And Effectual Calling—"The Holy Spirit effectually calls all the elect to repent and believe." Dagg demonstrates that Scripture clearly teaches that: "God has an elect or chosen people," Christ has a "peculiar people in view" when he purchases their redemption, and the "gospel calls all who hear it to repent and believe," but only those who receive an "internal and effectual" call, which "always produces repentance and faith" can obey the gospel call.[84]

J. P. Boyce's 1887 *Abstract of Systematic Theology* was the next major Southern Baptist work in the field. He includes chapters on election, reprobation, outward and effectual calling, regeneration and conversion, repentance, faith, and justification. He states that

> election is:
> (1.) An act of God, and not the result of the choice of the elect.
> (2.) That this choice is one of individuals, and not of classes.
> (3.) That it was made without respect to the action of the persons elected.
> (4.) By the good pleasure of God.
> (5.) According to an eternal purpose.
> (6.) That it is an election to salvation and not to outward privileges.[85]

He shows from Scripture that "election took place before man's existence, or before the world began."[86] He indicates that there are

> four points involved in the decrees as to Reprobation:
> 1. The decree not to elect.

---

[84] Dagg, *Manual of Theology, First Part*, 309, 324, 331–32.

[85] James Petigru Boyce, *Abstract of Systematic Theology* (1887; repr., Bellingham, WA: Logos Bible Software, 2010), 348.

[86] Boyce, 353.

2. The decree to pass by in bestowing divine grace.
3. To condemn for sins committed.
4. To harden against the truth all or some persons, already sinners, and to confirm them in sin.[87]

Boyce affirms that the "Gospel is, therefore, commanded to be proclaimed to every creature." Yet, this external call "meets with no success because of the wilful sinfulness of man." Therefore, only the effectual "influences of the Spirit … will lead to their acceptance of the call."[88] He continues, "[T]he Scriptures also teach that regeneration is the work of God, changing the heart of man by his sovereign will, while conversion is the act of man turning towards God with the new inclination thus given to his heart."[89] He concludes that "Christian repentance … involves a change in the outward life because such change is a result of the change of inward opinions."[90] "The seat of true repentance is in the soul, … not … mere intellectual knowledge, [and] the author of true repentance is God," writes Boyce.[91] "Christian faith," he states, "is personal reliance upon Christ for salvation because of belief of God's testimony as to our sinful and ruined condition, and as to what Christ has assuredly done to save us."[92]

He concludes that justification is "a judicial act of God" whereby he accepts the meritorious work of Christ as a substitute.[93] Thus, the ground of justification is the imputation of "the meritorious work of Christ."[94] Faith "has in it no merit in itself, but … seizes upon merit in" Christ, and works "manifest that justification has taken place, because they are invariable consequents." Justification results in "freedom from the condemnation of the law," "forgiveness of all sin," discharge from bondage to the law, and "peace with God."[95]

From their own words, it is clear that these two significant figures in the first fifty years of Southern Baptist life held to the Calvinistic theology of their Puritan forefathers. Moreover, Boyce gives evidence that these views were still predominant in the final decades of the nineteenth century.

---

[87] Boyce, 356.

[88] Boyce, 367–68.

[89] Boyce, 374.

[90] Boyce, 383.

[91] Boyce, 384.

[92] Boyce, 386.

[93] Boyce, 395.

[94] Boyce, 397.

[95] Boyce, 401–2.

When the biblical model of conversion is understood, a person's methodology will reflect it. They will communicate the gospel honestly, urgently, and confidently. They do this because they know that "it is the power of God for salvation to everyone who believes" (Romans 1:16).

Knowing that God is in control is freeing. The results are left to God to save whom he will, as the Spirit blows where it wills (John 3:8). The burden is not on the one presenting the gospel, nor on whether their presentation of the gospel was convincing. Instead, those who trust in the sovereignty of God in salvation are content to present the gospel, often on an ongoing basis, to a person and pray for the Spirit to grant them a new heart.

4

FINNEY'S REJECTION OF REFORMED ORTHODOXY

Finney's theological presuppositions inevitably led to his particular views of conversion and his subsequent methodology. Karl Dahlfred states that "Finney represents an Arminian point of view." [96] To the contrary, Martyn Lloyd-Jones says that, in fact, "Finney was not an Arminian; he was a Pelagian. He did not believe in original sin, and he believed that the natural man, by a process of reason, was able to grasp the truth and to put it into operation."[97] To be fair, Dahlfred later states that "Finney's views are strikingly similar to Pelagius' that grace is 'purely an external aid provided by God' and that there is 'no room for any special interior action of God upon the soul.'"[98]

Similarly, one should note that Dr. Lloyd-Jones does call Finney an Arminian in other places. Thus, Dahlfred's description is not entirely inaccurate but probably does not go far enough. Dr. Lloyd-Jones rightly points out the shortsightedness of these labels. He says that people often claim that,

> If men like Wesley and Finney and other Arminians can be involved in revival and used in it, well, we ought to be suspicious of revival. The mistake here is that we all tend to think in terms of labels and parties, not realizing that God displays

---

[96] Karl Dahlfred, *Theology Drives Methodology: Conversion in the Theology of Charles Finney and John Nevin* (Monee, IL: Createspace, 2012), 4.

[97] David Martyn Lloyd-Jones, "Living the Christian Life," in *The Puritans: Their Origins and Successors: Addresses Delivered at the Puritan and Westminster Conferences 1959–1978* (Edinburgh: Banner of Truth Trust, 2016), 314–15.

[98] Dahlfred, *Theology Drives Methodology*, 47.

> His sovereignty often in this way, that though a man may be muddled in his thinking … at certain points, God may nevertheless bless him and use him.[99]

In his *Memoirs,* Finney recounts the theological views of his Presbyterian mentor, Rev. George W. Gale, and then rejects them:[100]

> He held to the Presbyterian doctrine of original sin, or that the human *constitution* was morally depraved. He held also that men were utterly unable to comply with the terms of the Gospel, to repent, to believe, or to do anything that God required them to do. That while they were free to all evil, in the sense of being able to commit any amount of sin, yet they were not free in regard to all that was good. That God had condemned men for their sinful *nature,* and for this, as well as for their transgressions, they deserved eternal death, and were under condemnation. He held also that the influences of the Spirit of God on the minds of men *were physical,* acting directly upon the substance of the soul. That men were passive in regeneration, and in short he held all those doctrines that logically flow from the fact of a nature *sinful in itself.* These doctrines I could not receive. I could not receive his views on the subject of Atonement, regeneration, faith, repentance, the slavery of the will, or any of their kindred doctrines.[101]

Finney rejects a number of the core doctrines of Reformed orthodoxy here. Each of these rejections will be assessed in detail below.

In the preface to his *Systematic Theology,* if one can rightly call it that, Finney categorically rejects most of the Reformed doctrines of his denomination:

> I inquired in what sense the terms "regeneration," "faith," "repentance," "love," etc., were used but could obtain no answer, at which it did not appear to me that both reason and revelation revolted. The doctrines of a nature, sinful *per se,* of a necessitated will, of inability, and of physical regeneration, and physical Divine influence in regeneration, with their kindred and resulting dogmas, embarrassed and even confounded me at every step. I often said to myself, "If these things are taught in the Bible, I must be an infidel." But the more I read my Bible, the more clearly I saw that these things were not found there upon any fair principles

---

[99] David Martyn Lloyd-Jones, "Revival: An Historical and Theological Survey," in *The Puritans: Their Origins and Successors: Addresses Delivered at the Puritan and Westminster Conferences 1959–1978* (Edinburg: Banner of Truth Trust, 2016), 10.

[100] It should be noted that the critical edition, Charles G. Finney, *The Memoirs of Charles G. Finney: The Complete Restored Text*, ed. Garth M. Rosell and Richard A. G. Dupuis (Grand Rapids: Zondervan, 1997), which contains the unedited and unredacted text directly from Finney's original manuscripts, has been selected, rather than the popular edition, Charles G. Finney, *Memoirs of Rev. Charles G. Finney* (New York: A.S. Barnes, 1876), which was prepared by Oberlin College president, James Harris Fairchild. This original version has been redacted and omits many of the more objectional parts of Finney's theology and commentary on the events of his career.

[101] Finney, *Memoirs of Finney: Restored*, 48 (emphasis original).

> of interpretation, such as would be admitted in a court of justice.... The distinction between original and actual sin, and the utter absence of a distinction between physical and moral depravity, embarrassed me.... [They] speak of regeneration as consisting in anything but a voluntary change, and of Divine influence in regeneration, as anything but moral or persuasive.... Especially do I urge, to their logical consequences, the two admissions that the will is free, and that sin and holiness are voluntary acts of the mind.[102]

In Finney's legal mind, belief must be based on what is logical and capable of proof in a court of law. Due to his interpretational assumption that the creature must be able to comprehend the plans of the Creator fully, he could not find these things in the Bible. Therefore, he concluded that these doctrines could not be correct.

Contrary to Finney, Scripture states that man's heart is wicked and so deceitful that no one can know it (Jeremiah 17:9). Thus, it is absurd to think that one can rely on their observations of what is admissible *in a court of justice.* This teaching is in opposition to the teaching of Scripture. Instead, one must rely on what God has revealed in His Word. Scripture says that the way of salvation through a crucified Christ is "foolishness" to some and a "stumbling block" to others (1 Corinthians 1:23).

Further, Scripture tells us that God's thoughts are not our thoughts, and His ways are higher than ours (Isaiah 55:8–9). In fact, they are past finding out (Romans 11:33, see also Deuteronomy 29:29). Trying to take things to *their logical consequences* from man's perspective and reasoning is to try to satisfy the depraved mind of man. Yet this will not conform to God's revealed truth in His Word.

Commenting on the Westminster Assembly and the standards that it produced, Finney states: "That the instrument framed by that assembly should in the nineteenth century be recognized as the standard of the church, or of an intelligent branch of it, is not only amazing, but I must say that it is highly ridiculous."[103] This statement clearly shows the ascendancy of man in Finney's thought process and theology, which is in direct contrast to the descent of man since the Fall, as portrayed in the Bible. This is a theme that will lead to an anti-theological atmosphere in the decades to come, one that will depend more on man's intellect rather than the Word of God as the final arbiter. In his *Memoirs,* Finney recounts being examined by the presbytery to be licensed to preach. They asked if he "received the Confession of faith of

---

102 Charles G. Finney, *Finney's Systematic Theology*, ed. J. H. Fairchild, Abridged (1846–1847; repr., Minneapolis: Bethany Fellowship, 1976), ix, x; Similarly, he states to Rev. Gale in his *Memoirs,* "If there is nothing better than I find in your library to sustain the great doctrines taught by our church, I must be an infidel." (Finney, *Memoirs of Finney: Restored*, 55).

103 Finney, *Finney's Systematic Theology*, xii.

the Presbyterian church." He replied that he "received it for substance of doctrine, so far as [he] understood it," even though he "had not examined it."[104]

Rejection of Total Depravity

It is "absurd and impossible," Finney states, that "some physical pollution, transmitted from Adam, through the agency of God or the devil, which is in itself sinful, and deserving of the wrath of God, previous to the voluntary agency on the part of the sinner" is behind man's will "and the cause of all actual transgression."[105] To the contrary, Charles Hodge demonstrates that the leading confessions of the Reformation era define original sin as "a corrupted nature—or hereditary taint derived from Adam, propagated by ordinary generation, infecting the whole race, and the source or root of all actual sin."[106] The evidence is clear that Finney's views contradict Reformed orthodoxy and the explicit teaching of Scripture (See Romans 5:12–19; 1 Corinthians 15:21–22, 45, 49).

Albert B. Dod reviewed Finney's *Lectures on Revival of Religion* and *Sermons on Various Subjects* in an 1835 article. He rightly summarizes Finney's views when he states, "Mr. Finney denies that there is any such thing as *natural depravity*. His views on this subject are easily exhibited. We might describe them all, indeed, in a single phrase, by saying, that they are neither more nor less than the old Pelagian notions."[107]

Rejection of Total Inability

Finney displays his Pelagian beliefs when discussing the doctrine of man's inability to respond to the gospel without the effectual call of the Holy Spirit. He asserts that man was not as affected by the fall as Calvinists state. He claims: "It slanders God so, charging him with infinite tyranny, in commanding men to do that which they have no power to do.... It is not

---

[104] Finney, *Memoirs of Finney: Restored*, 53–54.

[105] Charles G. Finney, "Total Depravity," in *Sermons on Important Subjects* (New York: John S. Taylor, 1836), 136–37.

[106] Charles Hodge, "The New Divinity Tried. Review of 'the New Divinity Tried;' or, an Examination of the Rev. Mr. Rand's Strictures on a Sermon Delivered by the Rev. C. J. Finney, on Making a New Heart by C. J. Finney," *The Biblical Repertory and Theological Review* IV, no. 1–4 (1832): 290.

[107] Albert B. Dod, "Lectures on Revivals of Religion and Sermons on Various Subjects," *The Biblical Repertory and Theological Review*, New Series, 7, no. 1–4 (1835): 504 (emphasis original).

because they *cannot* do what God commands, but because they are *unwilling.*"[108]

In stark disagreement with Finney, the Bible teaches that no man can, nor will, come to Christ unless the Father draws him (John 6:44). Scripture is clear that no one seeks God (Romans 3:11). Therefore, the natural man is both unable and unwilling to come to God without a supernatural work of the Holy Spirit on the heart. Answering Finney's objection, Albert Dod states:

> [The] Bible does not inform us that there is any tyranny in God's commanding men to do what they cannot do. It teaches us directly the contrary, by making known the duty of man to receive the things of the Spirit of God, while it at the same time declares, that without divine assistance he *cannot* receive or know them.[109]

Finney's man-centered anthropology was the foundation of his theology. He writes, "It is a dictate of reason, of conscience, of common sense, and of our natural sense of justice, that if God require of us the performance of any duty or act, he is bound in justice to give us power to obey; i.e. he must give us the faculties and strength to perform the act."[110] Thus, if Scripture commands or tells what *ought* to be done, this implies power and ability to obey in Finney's system of theology. In Finney's system, God's moral government could not stand without this assumption. In contrast, Martin Luther stated,

> 'that by the words of the law man is admonished and instructed what he ought to do, not what he can do;' that is, to know his sin, not to believe that he has some power.... The words adduced are imperative, and only express what ought to be done. For Moses does not say, you have strength or power to choose, but 'choose, keep, do.' He delivers commands to do, but does not describe man's power of doing.... These injunctions, however, are not delivered unseasonably, or in vain; but are so many lessons by which vain and proud man may learn his own diseased state of impotency, if he try to do what is commanded.... Thus it is with the Scriptures also: what may be done in us by the power of God, and what we cannot do of ourselves, is declared by such like words.... Each of these

---

[108] Charles G. Finney, *Lectures on Revivals of Religion* (New York: Fleming H. Revell, 1888), 197 (emphasis original).

[109] Dod, "On Revivals of Religion," 519 (emphasis original).

[110] Charles G. Finney, "Sinners Bound to Change Their Own Hearts," in *Sermons on Important Subjects* (New York: John S. Taylor, 1836), 25.

two things is couched under this trope: namely, that, on the one hand we can do nothing of ourselves; and on the other, whatever we do, God worketh it in us.[111]

One can see the inconsistency in Finney's argument when he states: "People often *desire* to be Christians when they are wholly unwilling to be so.... [Being] WILLING to obey Christ is to be a Christian. When an individual actually *chooses* to obey God, he is a Christian. But all such desires, as do not imply actual choice are nothing."[112] In Finney's theological system, if God desires something to happen, He is obligated to give man the ability to carry that out. However, according to Scripture, no one wants to be a Christian unless their heart is first supernaturally changed by God (Ezekiel 36:26).

The fact that God commands all men everywhere to repent and believe (Mark 1:15, Acts 17:30) does not imply that they have the ability or willingness to do so. Finney's rational logic appears to be one-sided. He has a different standard for God than for man. He claims that God must give what He commands, but man does not necessarily have to be able to do what he desires. In fact, man may voluntarily remain unwilling to do what God requires. Addressing just such an objection, Archibald Alexander states:

> It will be objected, with much confidence, that if man has no ability to repent, he cannot be blamed for not repenting. But this is only true, if he desires to repent, and is unable to do it. This, however, is not the case of the impenitent sinner. He does not wish to repent—if he did, there is no hindrance in his way. But his soul is at enmity with God, and this opposition is so deep and total that he has neither the will nor the power to convert himself to the love of God.[113]

Man's dependence on the sovereignty of God and inability to save himself is flatly rejected as absurd by Finney in his *Lectures on Revivals of Religion.* Albert B. Dod, in his review, cites numerous examples of this and then satirically concludes:

> What can be more evident than that Mr. Finney considers himself a great reformer. He comes forth with the avowed purpose of clearing away the errors by which the true gospel has been so overlaid as to destroy its efficiency. He

---

[111] Martin Luther, *Martin Luther on the Bondage of the Will; to the Venerable Mister Erasmus of Rotterdam, 1525*, trans. Edward Thomas Vaughan (London: T. Hamilton, 1823), 164, 166, 210, 211.

[112] Finney, *Lectures on Revivals of Religion*, 357–58 (emphasis original).

[113] Archibald Alexander, "An Inquiry into That Inability Under Which the Sinner Labours, and Whether It Furnishes Any Excuse for His Neglect of Duty," *The Biblical Repertory and Theological Review*, New Series, III, no. 1–4 (1831): 380.

> comes to declare new truths, as well as to unfold new methods of presenting them to the mind.[114]

It is actually Finney that obscured the true gospel and preached *another gospel.*

Rejection of Unconditional Election

Concerning the doctrine of election, Finney states: "The elect must be those whom God foresaw could be converted under the wisest administration of his government.… [H]e foresaw that certain individuals could with the wisest amount of moral influence be reclaimed and sanctified, and for this reason they were chosen to eternal life."[115] Robert Caldwell summarizes Finney's position: "God executes his work of election in the following way. In his infinitely comprehensive knowledge of the universal whole, he knew who *could* be converted and consequently brings sufficient moral influence into their lives to influence them to conversion."[116] B. B. Warfield concludes that for Finney: "God elects those whom He *can* save, and leaves unelected those whom He *cannot* save, consistently with the system of government which He has determined to establish as the wisest and best."[117] In contrast, Scripture says, "In love [God the Father] predestined us for adoption as sons through Jesus Christ, *according to the purpose of his will*, to the praise of his glorious grace" (Ephesians 1:4–6, emphasis added) and "In him we have obtained an inheritance, having been predestined according to the purpose of him who works all things *according to the counsel of his will*" (Ephesians 1:11, emphasis added).

Scripture states that "those whom [God the Father] foreknew he also predestined to be conformed to the image of his Son … and those whom he predestined … he also justified" (Romans 8:29–30). Nowhere does Scripture say that God foresaw those whom he would convert beforehand. On the contrary, it states that those God the Father foreknew or lovingly and graciously selected, He predestined to be conformed to the image of His Son. Scripture does not limit God to only providing salvation to those He thought could be convinced to love Him. Scripture states that the Father loved, or foreknew, those He wanted to conform to the image of His Son and thus ensured that they would be justified.

---

114 Dod, "On Revivals of Religion," 485.

115 Charles G. Finney, "Doctrine of Election," in *Sermons on Important Subjects* (New York: John S. Taylor, 1836), 213–14.

116 Robert W. Caldwell III, *Theologies of the American Revivalists: From Whitefield to Finney* (Downers Grove, IL: InterVarsity Press, 2017), 173.

117 Benjamin Breckinridge Warfield, "Oberlin Perfectionism," *The Princeton Theological Review* XIX, no. 1–4 (1921): 572 (emphasis original).

Rejection of Limited Atonement

Finney denies the substitutionary nature of the atonement and instead propounds what is known as the moral government theory.[118] Finney describes moral government as God's government of moral beings by enlightening their minds about what is right and the consequences of wrong action.[119] Soon after being converted, Finney "had a long conversation with [his pastor] on the Atonement."[120] He recounts,

> He was a Princeton student, and of course held the limited view of the Atonement—that it was made for the elect and available to none else.… He held that Jesus suffered for the elect the literal penalty of the divine law—that He suffered just what was due to each of the elect on the score of retributive justice. I objected that this was absurd, as in that case He suffered the equivalent of endless misery multiplied by the whole number of the elect. He insisted that this was true. He affirmed that Jesus literally paid the debt of the elect, and fully satisfied *retributive* justice. On the contrary it seemed to me that Jesus only satisfied *public* justice and that that was all that the government of God could require. I was however but a child in theology.[121]

Every aspect of theology must hold up to Finney's logical scrutiny or be rejected as *absurd,* regardless of what Scripture states. In his *Memoirs,* Finney says he "was confident that [graduates of Princeton] had been wrongly educated."[122] By this, he meant that the Reformed orthodoxy taught by Princeton was incorrect because it did not conform to his man-centered system.

In Finney's system of theology, "Atonement is an exhibition of God suffering as a substitute for his rebellious subjects."[123] Caldwell says that for Finney, "God remains holy in relaxing the strictness of the law and extending

---

118 GOVERNMENTAL ATONEMENT A view about the death of Jesus Christ that says that Christ, by his death on the cross, simply fulfilled God the Father's requirement of punishment for sin, making it possible for people to save themselves by believing and becoming holy. ("A Glossary of Terms," *Christian History Magazine*, no. 20: Charles Finney: American Revivalism [1988]: 25, https://christianhistoryinstitute.org/uploaded/50cf76f3653009.10451180.pdf).

119 J. H. Fairchild, "Glossary," in *Finney's Systematic Theology*, Abridged (1846–1847; repr., Minneapolis: Bethany Fellowship, 1976), 430.

120 Finney, *Memoirs of Finney: Restored*, 44.

121 Finney, 44 (emphasis original); "This was the governmental theory of the Atonement, as it came to be called" Finney, 44n5.

122 Finney, *Memoirs of Finney: Restored*, 47.

123 Charles G. Finney, *Lectures on Systematic Theology: Embracing Lectures on Moral Government, Together with Atonement, Moral and Physical Depravity, Regeneration, Philosophical Theories, and Evidences of Regeneration*, vol. 1 (Oberlin, OH: Fitch, 1846), 409.

pardon, because in the public sufferings of Christ the law's demands have been satisfied."[124] "[Finney's] theory is substitutionary not because Christ pays for the actual sins of sinners, but because the public display of his suffering honors the moral law. Thus his atoning work serves as a substitute for their eternal judgment," summarizes Caldwell.[125] Yet Finney claimed that "it was easy to prove that the Atonement was made for *all mankind*."[126]

Rejection of Imputed Righteousness

Finney claims that "gospel justification, or justification by faith, consists in *pardon and acceptance with God*" such that "men are justified by faith and holiness." This faith is not on "the ground of the law." Instead, "they are *treated as if* they were righteous, on account of their faith and works of faith." He asserts that "sinners are pardoned, and accepted, and justified" if they "repent, believe, and become holy." Only then will "their past sins be forgiven, for the sake of Christ."[127] These statements clearly show the Pelagian works-based foundation of Finney's system.

Finney states that the imputation of Christ's righteousness to sinners is "absurd and impossible." He says that "Gospel Justification is not the imputed righteousness of Jesus Christ. Under the gospel, sinners are not justified by having the obedience of Jesus Christ set down to their account, as if he had obeyed the law for them, or in their stead."[128] Scripture, however, makes a very different claim. It says, "For our sake he made him to be sin who knew no sin, so that in him we might become the righteousness of God" (2 Corinthians 5:21).

In his *Memoirs,* Finney states that he "could not receive that theological *fiction* of *imputation*" that "Brother Gale" taught.[129] He summarizes Gale's position as follows:

> [H]e maintained that the guilt of Adam's first transgression is literally imputed to all his posterity; … that we received from Adam, by natural generation, a nature wholly sinful and morally corrupt in every faculty of soul and body, [and] that we are all justly condemned and sentenced to eternal damnation for our own unavoidable transgression of the law.… Then the second branch of this wonderful imputation is as follows: The sin of all the elect, both original and

---

124 Caldwell, *Theologies of the American Revivalists*, 175.

125 Caldwell, 175.

126 Finney, *Memoirs of Finney: Restored*, 51.

127 Charles G. Finney, "Justification by Faith," in *Lectures to Professing Christians* (New York: John S. Taylor, 1837), 217.

128 Finney, 215.

129 Finney, *Memoirs of Finney: Restored*, 59.

> actual—that is, the guilt of Adam's sin, so far as the elect are concerned, together with the guilt of their sinful nature, and also the guilt of their personal transgressions, are all literally imputed to Christ.
>
> The third branch of this wonderful *theological fiction* is as follows: First, the obedience of Christ to the divine law is literally imputed to the elect, … Secondly, His death for them is also imputed to the elect, so that in Him they are regarded as having fully suffered … Thirdly, thus by their surety the elect have first perfectly obeyed the law.
>
> I found it impossible to agree with Mr. Gale on these points. I could not but regard and treat this whole question of imputation as a theological fiction.

Finney's rejection of the Bible's clear teaching on the nature of the atonement is evident in these statements.

Rejection of Irresistible Grace

As noted above, Finney was "embarrassed" by the idea of "physical regeneration, and physical Divine influence in regeneration."[130] Finney's sermon entitled "Traditions of the Elders" states: "[T]he dogma of *physical regeneration,* [is necessary] if the *nature itself* be depraved; if depravity is *constitutional* … then regeneration must be physical. It must remedy the defect in the constitution."[131] He then proceeds to reject this orthodox view. He states that

> what is generally called irresistible grace … maintains that sinners are irresistibly converted.… By irresistible grace *I* understand and mean nothing more than that it is not, in [the case of the elect], resisted. But it has been maintained by some that it was properly irresistible. This is evidently a limb of physical regeneration. But what is more calculated to quiet a man in his sins, than the idea of irresistible grace in regeneration.… I cannot think of a sentiment more directly calculated to break the power of the gospel, to strengthen the sinner's hands in his rebellion, and settle him quietly down upon his lees until he sinks to the depths of hell.… The inference from their premises was irresistible, that they must wait, and consequently a compromise ensured; instead of calling upon him, and insisting upon his immediate repentance; instead of urging him to make to him a new heart and a new spirit, on pain of eternal death, he has been told to pray, to use the means, to call upon God for influences of his spirit and wait for sovereign grace to change his heart.[132]

---

130 Finney, *Finney's Systematic Theology*, ix.

131 Charles G. Finney, "Traditions of the Elders," in *Sermons on Important Subjects* (New York: John S. Taylor, 1836), 71 (emphasis original).

132 Finney, 71 (emphasis original).

Finney only gives lip service to irresistible grace and the actions of the Holy Spirit in conversion. The deciding factor for him is that the person makes himself *a new heart and a new spirit.* On the contrary, God says, "I will give you a new heart and put a new spirit within you; and I will remove the heart of stone from your flesh and give you a heart of flesh" (Ezekiel 36:26).

In his *Memoirs,* Finney states,

> The doctrine that sin was constitutional and belonged to the very nature, that the very nature itself must be changed by direct physical influence exerted by the Holy Spirit, compelled ministers who believed it to remind sinners of their inability to do what God required.... [U]nder such preaching it was no wonder that few souls were converted. The Lord convinced me that this was no way to deal with souls. He showed me clearly that moral depravity must be *voluntary;* that the divine agency in regeneration must consist in teaching the soul, in argument, in persuasion, entreaty. That therefore the thing to be done was to set the sinner's duty clearly before him.[133]

Finney rejects two core doctrines here. First, moral depravity as a consequence of the fall, making conversion voluntary on man's part. Second, the direct physical influence exerted by the Holy Spirit, or what reformed orthodoxy would call irresistible grace in conversion.

In his Lectures on Systematic Theology, Finney states that

> Regeneration by the Holy Spirit through the truth illustrates the wisdom of God.... For if sinners are to be regenerated by the influence of truth, argument, and persuasion, then ministers can see what they have to do, and how it is that they are to be 'workers together with God.' ... Ministers should lay themselves out and press every consideration upon the attention of sinners.... They should aim at and expect the regeneration of sinners upon the spot and before they leave the house of God. Sinners must not wait for and expect physical omnipotence to regenerate them ... for regeneration is not effected by physical power.[134]

For Finney, regeneration is accomplished solely by the Holy Spirit applying truth to the mind. Then it is left up to the sinner, who according to Scripture is dead in his trespasses and sins (Ephesians 2:1), to make the right decision. He rejects the idea that God can put his law within the sinner and write it on his heart (Jeremiah 31:33) in the conversion process so that they want to do what they would never want to do otherwise. He considers this a *physical* act of regeneration. In a section on *What the provisions of grace are not,* Finney states:

> It has made no provisions to save any one who will not fulfill the conditions of salvation. It has made no provisions for the bestowment of irresistible grace, for the very terms imply a contradiction. A moral agent can not be *forced* or

---

133 Finney, *Memoirs of Finney: Restored,* 321 (emphasis original).

134 Finney, *Lectures on Systematic Theology,* 1846, 1:519–20.

> necessitated to act in any given manner, and still remain a moral agent. That is, he can not be a moral agent in any case in which he acts from *necessity*.[135]

In the section "What these provisions are," Finney states, "Grace has made sufficient provisions to render the salvation of all possible, and such as will actually secure the salvation of a portion of mankind."[136] For Finney, grace is only for those who *fulfill the conditions of salvation.* In other words, it is salvation by works rather than grace. Salvation is no longer by grace if there are requirements to *earn* salvation. Grace is, by definition, free (Romans 11:6).

It is clear that Finney either does not understand the reformed doctrine of irresistible grace or that he intentionally misrepresents it. The latter seems more probable. Scripture is clear that God does not *force* anyone to act contrary to their will. Instead, God's "people shall be willing in the day of [his] power" (Psalm 110:3 KJV). They will not need to be coerced against their will because when God grants them a new heart, they will delight in doing His will (Psalm 40:8 ESV).

Rejection of Perseverance of the Saints

In a sermon entitled "Sinners Bound To Change Their Own Hearts," Finney states,

> The constitutional implantation of a principle of holiness in the mind, or the creation of a constitutional taste for holiness, if such a thing were possible, would render the perseverance of the saints physically necessary, making falling from grace a natural impossibility, and would thus destroy all the virtue of perseverance.[137]

For Finney, perseverance is a virtue. It is something that man must do to maintain a right standing with God rather than something that God does by preserving those whom he has drawn to himself. In a section of his *Lectures on Systematic Theology* entitled "State what is not intended by the perseverance of the saints, as I hold the doctrine," Finney writes:

> It is not intended that any sinner will be saved without complying with the conditions of salvation; that is, without regeneration and persevering in obedience to the end of life.... It is not intended that saints or the truly regenerate can not fall from grace and be finally lost by natural possibility.... It is not intended that the true saints are in no danger of apostasy and ultimate

---

[135] Charles G. Finney, *Lectures on Systematic Theology: Embracing Ability (Natural, Moral and Gracious) Repentance, Impenitence, Faith and Unbelief*, vol. 2 (Oberlin, OH: Fitch, 1847), 329 (emphasis original).

[136] Finney, 2:330.

[137] Finney, "Sinners Bound to Change Their Own Hearts," 6.

> damnation.... It is not intended that the salvation of the saints is possible except upon condition of great watchfulness, and effort, and perseverance on their part.... It is not intended that their salvation is certain in any higher sense than all their future free actions are.[138]

Finney, once again, gives lip service to orthodox doctrine but denies it when he states the doctrine as *he* holds it. Finney seems to intentionally redefine the doctrine to keep it in name only and reject it as traditionally held in reformed orthodoxy. J. I. Packer states the orthodox position as follows:

> Let it first be said that in declaring the eternal security of God's people it is clearer to speak of their *preservation* than, as is commonly done, of their perseverance. Perseverance means persistence under discouragement and contrary pressure. The assertion that believers persevere in faith and obedience despite everything is true, but the reason is that Jesus Christ through the Spirit persists in *preserving* them.[139]

This doctrine of the church has always been held and comforted the saints amidst many trials. There is no peace in a system where one's salvation relies on what one does rather than what Christ has done for them.

Summary of Finney's Rejection of Orthodoxy

Like Dr. Lloyd-Jones many years before, Horton states, "Finney is not merely an Arminian, but a Pelagian. He is not only an enemy of Protestantism, but of historic Christianity of the broadest sort."[140] Horton accurately summarizes Finney's unorthodox beliefs. He states that for Finney: "God is not sovereign; man is not a sinner by nature; the atonement is not a true payment for sin; justification by imputation is insulting to reason and morality; the new birth is simply the effect of successful techniques; and revival is a natural result of clever campaigns."[141] Warfield concludes, "It is quite clear that what Finney gives us is less a theology than a system of morals. God might be eliminated from it entirely without essentially changing its character. All virtue, all holiness, is made to consist in an ethical determination of will."[142]

---

[138] Finney, *Lectures on Systematic Theology*, 1847, 2:516–17.

[139] J. I. Packer, *Concise Theology: A Guide to Historic Christian Beliefs* (Wheaton, IL: Tyndale House, 1993), 241 (emphasis added).

[140] Horton, "The Legacy of Charles Finney," 9.

[141] Horton, 9.

[142] Warfield, "Oberlin Perfectionism," 596.

5

SCRUTINY OF FINNEY'S THEOLOGY AND METHODOLOGY

The conversion theology and revival methodology popularized by Finney directly contributed to theological drift partly due to his rejection of the use of the means of grace. His man-centered soteriology and revivalism also contributed. In subsequent years evangelicalism would drift from Calvinism to Arminianism.

Rejection of the Use of the Means of Grace

In his *Memoirs,* Finney states that he labored between several congregations where:

> The practice had been, I believe universal, to set anxious sinners to praying for a new heart, and to using means for their own conversion. The directions they received either assumed, or implied, that they were very willing to be Christians, and were taking much pains to persuade God to convert them. I tried to make them understand that God was using the means with them, and not they with Him; that God was willing, and they were unwilling; that God was ready, and they were not ready. In short, I tried to shut them up to present faith and repentance as the thing which God required of them—present and instant submission to His will, present and instant acceptance of Christ. *I tried to show them that all delay was only an evasion of present duty; that all praying for a new heart, was only trying to throw the responsibility of their conversion upon God;* and that all efforts to do duty, while they did not give their hearts to God, were hypocritical and delusive, and no doing of duty at all.[143]

Finney is adamant that God is willing to save people, but they are unwilling to be saved. This statement is a biblically-consistent assertion since no one seeks after God (Romans 3:11). However, Finney problematically denies

[143] Finney, *Memoirs of Finney: Restored,* 80 (emphasis added).

man's moral inability and tells people that all they must do is repent and have faith. He describes this as their duty to do by their own power, while Scripture says that faith and repentance are gifts of God (Ephesians 2:8; Acts 11:18).

In his lecture entitled "False Comforts For Sinners," Finney states:

> It is false comfort to tell an anxious sinner to do anything for relief, *which he can do, and not submit his heart to God.* An anxious sinner is often willing to do anything else but the very thing which God requires him to do.... I will mention a few of the things which sinners are told to do.... Telling a sinner he must *use the means.* Tell an anxious sinner this—You must use the means, and he is relieved "Oh, yes, I will do that, if that is all. I thought that God required me to repent and submit to him now. But if using the means will answer, I will do that with all my heart. He was distressed before, because he was cornered up, and did not know which way to turn.... What is the sinners use of means, but rebellion against God?[144]

The following account from Jonathan Edwards directly refutes Finney's false understanding of the use of the means of grace. He states,

> [A]wakenings when they have first seized on persons, have had two effects; one was, that they have brought them immediately to quit their sinful practices.... The *other* effect was, that it put them on earnest application to the means of salvation, reading, prayer, meditation, the ordinances of God's house, and private conference; their cry was, *What shall we do to be saved?* The place of resort was, now altered, it was no longer the tavern, but the minister's house that was thronged far more than ever the tavern had been wont to be.[145]

Finney claims to follow the theological tradition of Jonathan Edwards. Caldwell points out that Finney's version of the Edwardsean tradition is often almost unrecognizable, mainly because of his alteration of the doctrines of original sin and total depravity. He reenvisions them to conform to his Pelagian view of man's ability to comply with God's requirements.[146] In contrast to Finney's position, Edwards presents the use of the means of grace as part of the Holy Spirit's preparation for salvation. Like others in the Puritan tradition, he understood that regeneration had often already occurred but was not yet evident to the one under conviction. The Spirit was striving with their spirit and had regenerated them before they recognized it as a

---

144 Finney, *Lectures on Revivals of Religion*, 327 (emphasis original).

145 Jonathan Edwards, "A Faithful Narrative of the Surprising Work of God, in the Conversion of Many Hundred Souls, in Northampton, and the Neighboring Towns and Villages of New Hampshire, in New England; in a Letter to the Rev. Dr. Colman, of Boston," in *The Works of Jonathan Edwards*, ed. Edward Hickman, vol. 1 (1834; repr., Edinburgh: Banner of Truth Trust, 1974), 350–51 (emphasis original).

146 Caldwell, *Theologies of the American Revivalists*, 7. See the section "Finney's Perversion of his Edwardsean Theological Inheritance" for further discussion on this point.

rightly states, "This is evidently another gospel."[156] Later in the same article, Dod states:

> There is no evidence that the perversion of the truth which Mr F. thinks can only be met by varying the manner in which the apostles represent man's dependence, is a modern error. On the contrary, it is undeniable that this very error prevailed in the days of the apostles.... [Paul] does not, nor does any one of the sacred writers, affirm in a single instance that the sinner is able to obey the divine commands. Not a text of Scripture can be found in which this is declared, while a multitude can be produced which explicitly and in so many words deny it.[157]

Lecture XI of his *Lectures on Revivals of Religion*, "A Wise Minister Will be Successful," has Proverbs 11:30 as its text. Here Finney clearly shows just how unorthodox and man-centered his views of conversion are. He states,

> If men were converted by an act of physical omnipotence, creating some new taste, or something like that, and if sanctification were nothing but the same physical omnipotence rooting out the remaining roots of sin from the soul, it would not require so much sagacity and skill to win souls.... But the truth is that regeneration and sanctification are to be effected by moral means—by argument and not by force.[158]

The success of a man's ministry, and thus his wisdom, is determined "by the *number* of cases in which he is successful in converting sinners," says Finney.[159] He continually mocks those who think "God is a sovereign" in conversion and revival and those who believe that "God alone can convert sinners."[160] Any unsuccessful minister is either not called to preach, trained improperly, or too wicked to do his duty. By success, Finney means his number of converts. "Men cannot do the devil's work more effectually than by preaching up the sovereignty of God, as a reason why we should not put forth efforts to produce revival," claims Finney.[161] On the contrary, Jonathan Edwards writes,

> I think I have found that no discourses have been more *remarkably blessed,* than those in which the doctrine of God's *absolute sovereignty,* with regard to the salvation of sinners, and his *just liberty,* with regard to answering the prayers, or succeeding the pains, of natural men, continuing such, have been insisted on. I never found so much immediate saving fruit, in any measure, of any discourses I

---

156 Dod, "On Revivals of Religion," 203.

157 Dod, 210.

158 Finney, *Lectures on Revivals of Religion*, 167.

159 Finney, 175 (emphasis original).

160 Finney, 20, 84.

161 Finney, 177.

> have offered to my congregation, as some from these words, Rom. 3:19. "That every mouth may be stopped;" endeavouring to show from thence, that it would be just with God for ever to reject and cast off mere natural men.[162]

Speaking of his theological controversy with his mentor, Rev. Gale, Finney states:

> [O]ur controversy always turned upon this as the foundation upon which all the rest rested. If man had a sinful nature, then regeneration must consist in a change of nature. If man's nature was sinful, the influence of the Holy Spirit that must regenerate him, must be *physical* and not *moral.* If man had a sinful nature, there was no adaptation in the Gospel to change his nature, and consequently no connection in religion between means and end. *I could not receive it.* I did not so understand my Bible, nor could he make me see that it was taught in the Bible. When I came to read the Confession of faith, and saw the passages that were quoted to sustain these peculiar positions, I was absolutely ashamed of it. I could not feel any respect for a document that would undertake to impose on mankind such dogmas as those.[163]

Finney denies any supernatural work in conversion, or as he terms it, *physical* influence. He was ashamed of the biblical truths expressed in the *Westminster Confession of Faith* because he rejected the truths of reformed orthodoxy, as discussed in the previous chapter.

Finney's man-centric conception of the conversion process is evident in the concluding remarks to his lecture "Directions to Sinners." He says, "If you undertake to make converts, without cutting up all their errors, and tearing away all their false hopes, you may make a host of hypocrites, or of puny, dwarfish Christians, always doubting, and easily turned back from a revival spirit, and worth nothing."[164] Finney concedes that the Holy Spirit must enlighten the mind before conversion can occur. Yet, he clearly believes that the teaching of man makes a *useful* Christian. For him, the *errors* that must be cut up are the sovereignty of God in salvation and man's total inability to come to God without the effectual calling of the Holy Spirit. Although these are the clear teachings of Scripture, Finney categorically denies them. Thus, a *useful* Christian, in Finney's estimation, is one who, immediately after conversion, promotes the same man-centric version of revivalism and conversion that he taught. The following statement demonstrates the importance of this in his conversion theology:

> Where clear and discriminating instructions are given to convicted sinners, if they do not soon submit, their convictions will generally leave them. Convictions in

---

162 Edwards, "A Faithful Narrative," 353 (emphasis original).

163 Finney, *Memoirs of Finney: Restored*, 61 (emphasis original).

164 Finney, *Lectures on Revivals of Religion*, 361.

> such cases are generally short. Where sinners are deceived by false views, they may be kept along for weeks, and perhaps months, and sometimes for years, in a languishing state, and at last the truth is made clear to the sinner's mind, and all his errors are torn away, if he does not soon submit, his case is hopeless. Where the truth is brought to bear upon his mind, and he directly resists the truth that must convert him, there is nothing more to be done. The Spirit will soon leave him, for the very weapons he uses are resisted. Where instructions are not clear, and are mixed up with errors, the Spirit may strive even for years, in great mercy, to get sinners through the fog of false instruction. *But not so, where their duty is clearly explained to them, and they are brought right up to the single point of immediate submission,* and have all their false pretenses exposed, and the path of duty made perfectly plain. Then, if they do not submit, the Spirit of God forsakes them, and their state is well nigh hopeless.... It is this speculation, about the inability of sinners to obey God, that lays the foundation for all the protracted anguish and distress, and perhaps ruin, through which so many are led.[165]

In his *Memoirs,* Finney describes a time when he preached at the "stone schoolhouse at Evans' Mills." He recounts that he determined that he "could not spend [his] time with them unless they were going to receive the Gospel."[166] In Finney's own words, one sees that he believes that it is within the power of these individuals to immediately become Christians. He continues,

> I turned this question over, and pressed it upon them, and insisted upon it that I must know what course they proposed to pursue. If they did not purpose to become Christians, and enlist in the service of the Savior, I wanted to know it that I might not labor with them in vain. I said to them: "You admit that what I preach is the Gospel. You profess to believe it. Now will you *receive* it? Do you *mean* to receive it? Or do you intend to reject it? You must have some mind about it.
>
> After turning this over till I saw they understood it well, and looked greatly surprised at my manner of putting it, I then said to them: "Now I must know your minds. And I want that you who have made up your minds to become Christians, and will give your pledge to make your peace with God immediately, should rise up; but that on the contrary, those of you who are resolved that you will not become Christians, and wish me so to understand, and wish Christ so to understand, should sit still." After making this plain, so that I knew that they understood it, I then said: "You who now are willing to pledge to me and to Christ that you will immediately make your peace with God, please to rise up."[167]

Archibald Alexander addresses the consequence of such a rejection of man's inability:

---

165 Finney, 362–63 (emphasis added).

166 Finney, *Memoirs of Finney: Restored*, 65.

167 Finney, 65–66 (emphasis original).

> [W]hat is moral inability, but sin itself? It is the want of a right temper and a holy will—the defect of that love which the law requires; and what is this, but sin? ... Now what is called "moral inability," when it comes to be analysed, is nothing but the essence of sin, as it exists in the heart. Man labours under a moral inability to obey God, because he does not love him; but love is the sum and essence of all obedience; it is the same, therefore, as to say, that man, in his natural state, has no love to God. Man is in a state of sin, which, while it continues, must be an effectual hinderance to the service of God....
>
> These new preachers, in their addresses to the impenitent sinner, say nothing about natural and moral inability. They preach, that man is in possession of every ability which is requisite for the discharge of his duty. That it is as easy for him to repent, to exercise faith, and to love God, as to speak, or eat, or walk, or perform any other act.... Men, upon being assured that salvation is in their power, are induced to make an exertion to submit to God, and do often persuade themselves that now they have complied with their duty, and have passed from death unto life. There is much reason to fear, however, that many souls, who have very slight convictions of sin, are deluded into the opinion, that they have submitted, and are reconciled to God, though they have never been led to any deep views of the dreadful sinfulness of their own hearts.[168]

Thus we see that, contrary to the opinions of Finney, both conversion and revival are supernatural works of God. Sadly, many are still influenced by his man-centric approach today.

Finney's Perversion of his Edwardsean Theological Inheritance

Remarkably, Finney often quotes Jonathan Edwards in his lectures with much approval. He makes one believe that Edwards favors his views, even though Edwards is a staunch Calvinist and Finney is strongly anti-Calvinistic. Albert B. Dod states,

> [Finney produces] the names of a great number of wise and eminent men who have been prominent in introducing innovations. All this has nothing to do with the questions—it is perfectly puerile indeed to introduce it—unless these men introduced such innovations as he contends for. Among these new-measure men he introduces the name of President Edwards. And on several occasions he makes such a use of the name of this great man as is calculated to leave upon the reader's mind the impression that Edwards had sanctioned his proceedings. He has no right thus to slander the dead or impose upon the living.[169]

Caldwell accurately summarizes the relationship between Edwards's revival theology and Finney's. He states, "Jonathan Edwards contributed to the emergence of a new kind of Calvinism that in time gave rise to a revival

---

[168] Alexander, "Inquiry into That Inability," 370–71.

[169] Dod, "On Revivals of Religion," 253–54.

theology that was distinct from the moderate evangelicals.... [with] it's most extreme, and some would say *unrecognizable,* form in the revival theology of Charles Finney."[170]

Finney's rejection of man's moral inability as incompatible with the sinner's free will dramatically transformed his understanding of conversion from that of the Edwardsean theological tradition from which he inherited. This rejection caused him to emphasize the sinner's will as the ultimate deciding factor in the work of regeneration rather than God's sovereign choice and grace. Finney states, "There is nothing in religion beyond the ordinary power of nature. It is just that and nothing else. When mankind becomes religious, they are not *enabled* to put forth exertions which they were unable before to put forth."[171]

On the contrary, Edwards rightly states, "Conversion is a great and glorious work of God's power, at once changing the heart, and infusing life into the dead soul."[172] Finney's focus on freedom of the will led him to reenvision theological anthropology. He reshaped the doctrines of total depravity and original sin in unbiblical ways. He believed this would preserve man's liberty of choice.[173] Caldwell states that although the truth of original sin, which resulted in a corrupted human nature inherited from Adam, had been taught for generations, "Finney believed all this was rubbish."[174] Jay E. Smith concludes, "Finney's theology is primarily a system of morals based upon human effort with little need for God."[175]

Similarly, in the Baptist Faith and Message (BFM), one sees a subtle but significant change, which reflects the development of a more man-centric anthropology. In 1925 Article III, The Fall of Man, states that Adam's "posterity inherit a nature corrupt and in *bondage* to sin, are *under condemnation.*" Whereas, in 1963, Article III, Man, states that Adam's "Posterity inherit a nature and an environment *inclined* toward sin."[176] Contrary to Scripture, it denies that man is in bondage to sin due to being born with a sinful nature. Instead, it indicates that man's environment inclined toward sin is what influences him. "More significant," Tom Ascol states, "is the removal in 1963

---

[170] Caldwell, *Theologies of the American Revivalists*, 7 (emphasis added).

[171] Finney, *Lectures on Revivals of Religion*, 12 (emphasis original).

[172] Edwards, "A Faithful Narrative," 355.

[173] Caldwell, *Theologies of the American Revivalists*, 178.

[174] Caldwell, 179.

[175] Jay E. Smith, "The Theology Of Charles Finney: A System Of Self-Reformation," *Trinity Journal* 13, no. 1 (1992): 63, https://www.galaxie.com/article/trinj013-1-004.

[176] Southern Baptist Convention, "Comparison Chart – The Baptist Faith and Message," sbc.net, accessed December 18, 2021, https://bfm.sbc.net/comparison-chart/ (emphasis added).

of the idea that people are, because of their inherited sinful nature, 'under condemnation.'"[177] As with Finney, the BFM maintains orthodox terminology while subtly changing doctrine.

Pelagian and Semi-Pelagian Tendencies

A more detailed examination of Finney's Pelagian tendencies is warranted. Warfield states, "Pelagianism … is the instinctive thought of the natural man. But Finney's thought ran not merely into the general mold of Pelagianism, but into the special mold of the particular mode of stating Pelagianism which had been worked out by N. W. Taylor."[178] Taylor was part of the *New Haven* school of theology that took Edwardsean theology off in directions that Edwards himself never intended. Frank Foster declares, "Finney's system … may be dismissed in the one word 'Taylorism .'"[179]

The church condemned the heretical position espoused by Finney regarding the ability of man long ago. Archibald Alexander says,

> [A] council which met at Arles [in 314 A.D.] … denounced an anathema against the impious doctrines of Pelagius; and especially against the opinion *that man was born without sin; and that he could be saved by his own exertions.* They considered it a presumption worthy to be condemned for any man to believe that he could be saved without grace.[180]

Finney's views have much in common with the doctrine of the Roman Catholic Church, as set forth at the Council of Trent and defended by Andradius. Archibald Alexander summarizes the Roman Catholic position as follows:

> It is very evident, therefore, from the explicit declarations of this great defender of the council of Trent, how much they obscured and misrepresented this fundamental doctrine of scripture; and, accordingly, he finds great fault with a writer of his own church, who had taught, that from the soul infected with original sin no good thing could naturally proceed; asserting, that human nature

---

177 Thomas K. Ascol, *"Traditional" Theology & the SBC: An Interaction with, and Response to, The Traditional Statement of God's Plan of Salvation*, Revised Edition (Cape Coral, FL: Founders, 2018), 34.

178 Warfield, "Oberlin Perfectionism," 17.

179 Frank Hugh Foster, *A Genetic History of the New England Theology* (Chicago: University of Chicago Press, 1907), 467.

180 Archibald Alexander, "The Early History of Pelagianism," *The Biblical Repertory and Theological Review*, New Series, 2, no. 1–4 (1830): 89 (emphasis original).

> was not so entirely depraved, but that from it by proper discipline, some good thing might proceed *without the aid of grace.*[181]

Rome's view is the same Pelagian view of man's ability that Finney held. Martin Chemnitz (1522–1586) gives a summary of the opinions set forth at the Council of Trent that is equally applicable to Finney's view of original sin, "And when the mouth of the Lord speaks, all flesh ought to be silent, heaven and earth ought to give ear. But Andrada *prefers to hold an opinion with the Council of Trent rather than to believe with the Scripture.*"[182] Similarly, Finney would rather give weight to his opinion and reason than to the Word of God.

Backsliders or False Professors

In his lecture entitled "Backslider in Heart," Finney states that "backsliding in heart … consists in taking back that consecration to God and his service, that constitutes true conversion."[183] Throughout this lecture, his descriptions of the *backslider* more accurately portray the biblical description of the unregenerate false professor of religion, as described and warned against in Hebrews 6. Finney, once again, demonstrates his man-centered thought process and exposition of Scripture. He says that the backslider indicates in "his prayer that he is not in a state of Christian liberty—that he is having a 7th of Romans experience, instead of that which is described in the 8th of Romans."[184] Only a man-centered and Pelagian view of man and his ability to sanctify himself, or reach *perfection*, can conclude that Paul's description in Romans 7 is that of an unbeliever or *backslider*. A clear view of the depravity of man leads one to see that Paul is describing the constant struggle that believers face in battling the flesh in this life. This struggle will never be complete until our future glorification. Finney denies this fact and states, "I was satisfied that the doctrine of sanctification in this life, and entire sanctification in the sense that it was the privilege of Christians to live without known sin, was a doctrine taught in the Bible, and that abundant means were provided for the securing of that attainment."[185]

A. W. Pink sums up the biblical position, which is opposed to Finney, beautifully when he states:

---

[181] Archibald Alexander, "The Doctrine of Original Sin as Held by the Church, Both before and after the Reformation," *The Biblical Repertory and Theological Review*, New Series, 2, no. 1–4 (1830): 487 (emphasis added).

[182] Martin Chemnitz, *Examination of the Council of Trent*, trans. Fred Kramer, electronic ed., vol. 1 (St. Louis: Concordia, 1999), 328 (emphasis added).

[183] Finney, *Lectures on Revivals of Religion*, 412.

[184] Finney, 417.

[185] Finney, *Memoirs of Finney: Restored*, 393.

> [A] right conception of the sinner's will—its *servitude*—is essential to a just estimate of his depravity and ruin. The utter corruption and degradation of human nature is something which man hates to acknowledge, and which he will hotly and insistently deny until he is "taught of God." Much, very much, of the unsound doctrine which we now hear on every hand is the direct and logical outcome of man's repudiation of God's expressed estimate of human depravity.[186]

Scripture commands believers to strive to mortify the sins of the flesh (Romans 8:13) and teaches that one can only accomplish this through the enabling of the Holy Spirit. Even when regenerate, man cannot put away the deeds of the flesh in his own power. Supernatural help in the form of the indwelling of the Holy Spirit that comes with regeneration is required.

Finney states, "A sticklishness about forms, ceremonies, and non-essentials, is evidence of a backslidden heart."[187] It is tempting to agree with this statement. It is close to, yet so far from, the truth of Scripture. Scripture describes someone in this state as unregenerate. The Puritans would call him a *formal professor of religion.* One that gives mental assent to the truths of Scripture but has not truly been born again by the grace of God and became a new creation in Christ Jesus. Matthew Henry states, "[A] formal professor … flatters himself in his own eyes, doubts not of his salvation, is secure of heaven, and cheats the world with his vain confidences."[188] Similarly, John Gill writes, "[God] knows formal professors of religion, and upon what foot they have taken up their profession, and how they keep their lusts with their profession; he can distinguish between profession and grace."[189]

Finney's descriptions of the *backslider* refer to a man who is in just such a state, an unregenerate man, not a backslider. The man Finney describes is one who mentally assents to the truths of Scripture, which even the demons do and shudder, says James (2:19). Despite this, he is not in a saving relationship with Christ. Finney says that the "[backslider's] lustings [which] had been kept under … control … now resumed their control."[190] Finney believes a person controls his lustings by his own power rather than through the Holy Spirit's work, enabling him to manage his passions. Finney's

---

[186] Arthur W. Pink, *The Sovereignty of God*, Fourth Edition (Swengel, PA: Bible Truth Depot, 1949), 153 (emphasis original).

[187] Finney, *Lectures on Revivals of Religion*, 421.

[188] Matthew Henry, *Matthew Henry's Commentary on the Whole Bible: Complete and Unabridged in One Volume* (1706; repr., Peabody: Hendrickson, 1994), 672.

[189] John Gill, *An Exposition of the New Testament* (1763; repr., London: Mathews & Leigh, 1809), 3:396-397.

[190] Finney, *Lectures on Revivals of Religion*, 425.

description of this person as having "forsaken God" further evidences his misunderstanding of Scripture. In concluding remarks on "how to recover from a state of backsliding," he says, "Remember whence you are fallen. Take up the question at once, and deliberately contrast your present state with that in which you walked with God.... Repent at once, and do your first work over again.... Set yourself right with God."[191] In Finney's view, man's decision is always of utmost importance, not God's sovereign pleasure. Therefore, a person may choose God, later reject Him, and yet choose Him again. Thus, one's state of salvation depends on man's choice instead of Christ's finished work on the cross and God's preserving power of all those he draws to himself. Scripture unconditionally rejects Finney's view. It says one must examine their heart to see if they are in Christ (2 Corinthians 13:5).

Scripture does not tell one to examine themselves to see whether they have fallen away, but whether they ever were in Christ. John reminds his readers that some had gone out from among them because they never were true believers. If they were, they would have continued in Christ (1 John 2:19).

The author of Hebrews states that it would be "impossible to renew them again to repentance" (Hebrews 6:6) if they had truly believed and subsequently fallen from the faith. To do so would mean that Christ's finished work was insufficient to keep them in the faith. Christ would have to be crucified again. Suppose one's life evidences what Finney describes. In that case, one must scripturally conclude that they never indeed were in Christ and must now pray that God will grant them a new heart and the gifts of faith and repentance.

Finney's observation of these people is correct when he states, "Do not imagine yourself to be in a justified state, for you are not."[192] However, he wrongly comes to this conclusion based on the idea that this person was in a justified state previously, but now, due to his actions, he is no longer justified. On the contrary, Scripture states that those who genuinely believe will persevere because God will preserve them. Those who do not persevere were never justified in the first place. They had only fooled themselves and perhaps others around them, including those in the church, into believing they possessed the faith they professed to have.

Nothing New Under the Sun: Finney Only Propagates Error

Finney's theology was not new or innovative in and of itself. It was just heresies from days gone by, some of them ancient and some modern,

[191] Finney, 426–27.

[192] Finney, 427.

repackaged in a shiny wrapper. Caldwell states, "Though he is often regarded as a highly original maverick of nineteenth-century revivalism, Finney actually borrowed liberally from [Nathaniel] Taylor's thoughts."[193]

Finney was not the originator of the idea that regeneration is an act of moral suasion. However, he popularized it more than anyone before him. Jonathan Dickinson refuted this same error nearly one hundred years before Finney in a sermon titled "The Nature and Necessity of Regeneration," published in New York in 1743. He says,

> I know that there are some that call themselves Christians who pretend that this change is the effect of moral suasion only, and that it is only through the prevalence of outward means upon their minds that men are excited to become new creatures by the improvement of their natural abilities in the exercise of moral virtues and religious duties. According to them, the whole work of regeneration and progressive sanctification is but the improvement of those powers which are given in common to all that enjoy the ordinances of the Gospel. Although they will, in words, acknowledge our want of divine assistance in order to effect this change, they seem to allow no more of the peculiar and immediate influences of the blessed Spirit in this great concern than in the common and ordinary occasions of life. How loath are poor proud worms to give God the glory of His glorious free grace and divine operations! How willing they are to think well of themselves and, therefore, to slight and reproach all those experiences of the divine power upon the soul with which they themselves are unacquainted![194]

Likewise, Finney did not originate the altar call or *anxious bench* idea. However, he did help to bring it into common use. In a sketch of the life of Rev. Jeremiah Vardeman (1757–1842), Rev. John Mason Peck records that around 1800, Mr. Vardeman was preaching at a "social meeting" in rural Kentucky where:

> [B]efore they closed, he gave an invitation to all who felt conscious of their sinfulness and need of the power and grace of Christ, and who desired the prayers of God's people, to come forward and give him their hands, and he would offer special prayer to God in their behalf. This practice became very common, especially in seasons of revival, with most religious denominations through this Valley.... I have not been able to trace the practice beyond the social meeting

---

[193] Caldwell, *Theologies of the American Revivalists*, 125; "Nathaniel Taylor was the originator of New Haven Theology, which is also known as Taylorism, and precipitated New School Presbyterianism." Earl Wm. Kennedy, "Taylor, Nathaniel William (1786–1858)," in *Encyclopedia of the Reformed Faith*, ed. Donald K. McKim (Louisville, KY: Westminster John Knox, 1992).

[194] Jonathan Dickinson, "The Nature and Necessity of Regeneration," in *Salvation in Full Color: Twenty Sermons by Great Awakening Preachers*, ed. Richard Owen Roberts (1743; repr., Wheaton, IL: International Awakening, 1994), 138.

> described, of the people spontaneously moving forward and entreating the speaker to pray for them.[195]

Rev. James E. Welch indicates that Vardeman was "moderately Calvinistic" in doctrine while "in the habit of proposing to pray with" those under conviction. He states that he was careful to do no more than make the offer to pray for them.[196] Welch affirms that Vardeman

> never urged them forward, nor, as in modern times [*ca.* 1850], did he go through the congregation, persuading persons to occupy the 'anxious seats,' and by such means induce those under the influence of excited feelings, to make a profession of religion, and thus introduce into the church those whose zeal prompts them to 'run well for a time,' but passes away 'like the morning cloud and early dew.'[197]

It appears that asking people to come forward during the service was a relatively new and novel addition to religious services at the onset of the nineteenth century.

Summary

Finney set out to reject and oppose almost every tenet of Reformed Calvinistic orthodoxy. In the process of doing so, he supposed, in direct opposition to Scripture, that God is impotent and man is omnipotent. For Finney, Salvation depends on man's actions, and God does nothing more than provide moral suasion to help him choose the right and reject the wrong.

In 1995, Horton laid out an important question that is still before us twenty-five years later:

> It is always best, when one has lost something valuable, to retrace one's steps in order to determine when and where one last had it in his or her possession. That is the purpose of this exercise, to face with some honesty the serious departure from biblical Christianity that occurred through American revivalism. For until we address this shift, we will perpetuate a distorted and dangerous course. Of one thing Finney was absolutely correct: The Gospel held by the Westminster divines whom he attacked directly, and is indeed held by the whole company of evangelicals, is *"another gospel"* in distinction from the one proclaimed by Charles Finney. The question of our moment is, With which gospel will we side?[198]

This theological shift affected southern Baptists, as it did almost all other evangelicals. Indeed, many churches are still propagating *another gospel* that

---

195 Sprague, *Annals of the American Pulpit*, VI:422–23.

196 Sprague, VI:427.

197 Sprague, VI:427.

198 Horton, "The Legacy of Charles Finney," 8 (emphasis added).

does not take sin seriously today. It rejects the need for a life bearing the fruit of repentance as evidence of true conversion. It focuses on the *number of converts* rather than genuinely fulfilling the commission of Matthew 28:18–20. This commission requires Christians to make disciples and teach them to observe all Christ has commanded them to do. When God graciously saves a sinner, he obeys not to earn salvation but as a loving response to what God has done for him (Ephesians 2:8–10).

6

THE AFTERMATH OF FINNEY'S THEOLOGY AND METHODOLOGY

The effects of Finney's theology were recognized almost immediately by his contemporaries, many of whom attempted to sound the alarm. However, the seeming efficacy of Finney's man-centered approach won the day with subsequent generations. The consequences of his measures and theology are still alive and well within American evangelicalism. The reason for such long-lasting outcomes from one man's efforts, as will be seen, is due to a careful and deliberate rewriting of history.

The words of Asahel Nettleton, in a letter to Samuel Aiken concerning Finney's methods, dated January 13, 1827, seem almost prophetic when observed through the lens of history. David Porter, writing to Dr. Gardner Spring on May 28, 1827, states that this letter aimed to warn ministers against "the irregularities and confusion introduced into revivals at the West [which give] cause for alarm."[199] Nettleton writes,

> Those ministers and Christians who have heretofore been most and longest acquainted with revivals are most alarmed at the spirit which has grown out of the revivals of the west.... It is by keeping out and avoiding everything of this kind, that ... the character of revivals for *thirty* years past, has been guarded. If the evil be not soon prevented a generation will arise, inheriting all the obliquities of their leaders, not knowing that a revival ever did or can exist without all those evils. And these evils are destined to be propagated from generation to generation, waxing worse and worse.[200]

---

199 Gardiner Spring, *Personal Reminiscences of the Life and Times of Gardiner Spring, Pastor of the Brick Presbyterian Church, in the City of New York*, vol. 1 (New York: Charles Scribner, 1866), 235–36.

200 Bennet Tyler, *Nettleton and His Labours: Being the Memoir of Dr. Nettleton* (Edinburgh: T&T Clark, 1854), 344–48 (emphasis original).

A letter demonstrating that these effects were realized only two decades later was written by James W. Alexander to John Hall on December 31, 1846, which states:

> [T]here was great interest under the Finneyitish revivals, but it was not evangelical, and I am working among its bitter fruits every day. There is a wonderful vitality and permanency in experience which is built on the preaching of Christ.... When the new-divinity converts grow cold, they are colder than ice, nothing but a biting censoriousness. I had no idea, even in Jersey, of the modifications wrought in the city by the overwrought revivalism of past years.[201]

In another letter dated January 19, 1852, Alexander indicated that the city where he ministered had lived to see religious deterioration. He writes that this had fulfilled a "prediction made by Nettleton which at the time I thought absurd."[202] A sermon preached during the New York awakening of 1857–1858 on the confusion of revival and revivalism seems to confirm that Nettleton's prediction was not so absurd. He writes:

> We have not been faithful to the deposit with which we are entrusted. From the absurd attempt to keep up religion without doctrine, a large part of the present generation has grown up already, with no proper safeguard against soul-destroying error. Not only have they no tests to distinguish Pelagianism from Gospel grace, but they even learn to treat with indifference the heresies which deny the atonement and the godhead of Jesus.... The agency of the Holy Spirit has been cast into the shade: new and dangerous views of regeneration have become common; while the tendency has been away from dependence on God, and towards a religion of human fabrication.... At the same time that we were doing away with the true glory of revivals, even the sovereign agency of the Holy Spirit in changing the depraved nature, we were in some places laying mighty stress upon certain external means and measures.... All our difficulties in believing in the possibility of an unexampled increase of the church arise from our looking at human agency instead of divine efficiency. Perhaps one reason why God has so often arrested His bountiful hand, and left us to barrenness, is, that we have arrogated to ourselves much of the power. We have substituted man's work. We have taken regeneration out of God's hands into our own. We have made us new hearts, after the image of ourselves.[203]

The effects of this new theology and its associated measures are still evident in evangelicalism today. We often hear of people *planning* a revival as

---

[201] James Waddel Alexander, *Forty Years' Familiar Letters of James W. Alexander, D. D.: Constituting, with Notes, a Memoir of His Life*, ed. John Hall, vol. 2 (New York: Charles Scribner, 1860), 62.

[202] Alexander, 2:169.

[203] James Waddel Alexander, "The Holy Flock," in *The New York Pulpit in the Revival of 1858: A Memorial Volume of Sermons* (New York: Sheldon, Blakeman, 1858), 26–28, 31.

if it were something one could schedule at their convenience. Scripture indicates that revival is a supernatural work of God. He alone can bring revival about, on His own timetable, whenever and wherever He will without any help from man other than the secondary causes He foreordained before the world's foundation.

Finney's Polemical Rewriting of History

Murray demonstrates that Finney's *Memoirs* were a well-crafted polemic designed to push the new measures. He summarizes the extent of its success as follows:

> [I]n the 1860s Finney knew that it was not from theological lectures that the verdict of history would be drawn.... In the great purpose he had in view in 1866–8 everything that did not serve to strengthen his doctrinal crusade was put aside.... The thousands who have accepted it at face value have unwittingly accepted a reconstruction of history. While Christians in the 1830s and 1840s were not carried away by the new teaching to the extent that [modern writers] claim, there can be no question that by 1900 the impression was almost universal that Charles Grandison Finney had *introduced* revivals in nineteenth-century America and that his usefulness so exceeded that of all who went before him that there was little evangelistic endeavour before him that deserved attention. The belief has been repeated so often that is commonly regarded as unquestionable fact.[204]

Murray goes on to indicate the reasons for the acceptance of the new measures by so many:

> First, the claim that they were justified by massive success appeared so feasible that biblical warrant for their use seemed to be unnecessary. Scripture was not the decisive criterion.... Secondly, all Christians rightly want to *see* success, and the new measures seemed to offer that possibility in a way not known before. Thirdly, the introduction of the new measures in a time of real revival gave weight to the claim that their 'successes' were due to divine blessing. And, finally, the illusion was ultimately accepted because the alleged successes received far more publicity than did the evidence of harm done to the life of the churches.[205]

As will be shown, Finney's narrative is "historically indefensible" and "theologically untrue."[206] Nevertheless, it eventually won the day due to his careful rewriting of history in his *Memoirs*. Surprisingly, "Finney's Memoirs

---

204 Murray, *Revival and Revivalism*, 297–98 (emphasis original).

205 Murray, 298 (emphasis original).

206 Robert Pyke, "Charles G. Finney and the Second Great Awakening," *Reformation and Revival* 6, no. 1 (1997): 46, https://www.galaxie.com/article/rar06-1-03.

have not been out of print since the first edition of 1876." However, "the writings of the evangelical leaders of the Second Great Awakening," including numerous warnings against Finney's theology and methodology, have long since ceased to be printed.[207]

Conflation of Calvinism and Hyper-Calvinism

Finney considered anyone who held to the historic *five points* of Calvinism as a hyper-Calvinist. In fact, for Finney, hyper-Calvinism was redefined to mean Calvinism itself. Calvinism teaches that God is sovereign, yet man is responsible for his decisions. It also teaches that God uses frail creatures to promulgate the gospel, which is an incentive for evangelism. Finney falsely redefined a Calvinist as one who stresses God's sovereignty over man's responsibility to the extent that evangelism and missions are hampered or ignored. Tom Nettles states, "It is unfortunate that … definitions [of hyper-Calvinism] focus attention on 'Five-Point Calvinism' as somehow the same in essence with hyper-Calvinism.… The two elements … most pertinent for understanding hyper-Calvinism are the word *offer* and the statements concerning the responsibility of man."[208] Too much focus on the word *offer* tends towards Arminianism, and denying man's responsibility can lead to hyper-Calvinism. Finney's *Memoirs* contain numerous examples of this. He says that the preaching of his theological mentor at Adams, NY, Rev. Gale, "was of the Old School type, that is, it was thoroughly Calvinistic; and whenever he came out with the doctrines as he believed them, he would preach what is now called *hyper*-Calvinism."[209] On one occasion, he records,

> I have everywhere found that the peculiarities of hyper-Calvinism have been the stumbling block both of the church and of the world. A nature sinful in itself, a total inability to accept Christ and to obey God, condemnation to eternal death for the sin of Adam and for a sinful nature—and all the kindred and resultant dogmas of that peculiar school, have been the stumbling block of believers and the ruin of sinners.[210]

Similarly, when relating his efforts in England in 1850, Finney offhandedly remarks, "London is, and long has been, cursed with hyper-Calvinistic preaching."[211]

---

[207] Murray, *Revival and Revivalism*, 298.

[208] Nettles, *By His Grace*, 425 (emphasis original).

[209] Finney, *Memoirs of Finney: Restored*, 9 (emphasis original).

[210] Finney, 444.

[211] Finney, 506.

As stated above, Finney often claims to be following the Edwardsean tradition. Yet, he also makes bold and slanderous claims against Edwards's Calvinism to emphasize the need to promote his *new* measures:

> Hyper-Calvinistic views had obtained among Presbyterians and Congregationalists almost universally, up to the time that I began to preach. I saw that it was indispensable to introduce new views on several important questions, before anything like a successful effort could be made to convert the world. President Edwards' view of the bondage of the will, and the strange distinction he made between moral and natural ability and inability, had greatly influenced the ministry, and taken possession of nearly all the pulpits in the Presbyterian and Congregational denominations.
>
> In most of the Baptist churches in the country they held to a higher and more absurd Calvinism than in the Presbyterian and Congregational churches. It is not wonderful, therefore, that the theology which I preached should have excited alarm and resistance.[212]

Murray demonstrates that writers continued this trend after the turn of the twentieth century and "treat hyper-Calvinism and historic Calvinism as one and the same thing."[213] This misconception led to a common stereotype that is still present today. One which represents Calvinism as hostile to evangelism, which couldn't be further from the truth, as Particular Baptists in England were the first to send missionaries to India.[214] In 1955, George Washington Paschal called "the teaching in the Philadelphia Confession of Faith 'hyper-Calvinistic' and treats its influence as hostile to evangelism."[215] This polemic's effectiveness in decrying Calvinism as a hindrance to evangelism can also be seen in an entry on "Evangelism" in the *Encyclopedia of Southern Baptists*, written seventy-five years after Finney's death. It stated, "Finney has tremendously influenced Baptists as well as other evangelicals ... With his legal logic and Scripture texts, he refuted the extreme Calvinism which denied use of one's will and repentance or use of one's efforts to win others to Christ."[216] Yet, as Murray makes clear:

---

212 Finney, 536.

213 Murray, *Revival and Revivalism*, 315.

214 William Carey was the "Pioneer English Calvinistic Baptist missionary to India." (Duncan B. Forrester, "Carey, William (1761–1834)," in *Encyclopedia of the Reformed Faith*, ed. Donald K. McKim [Louisville: Westminster John Knox, 1992], 58).

215 George Washington Paschal, *History of North Carolina Baptists* (Raleigh: General Board, North Carolina Baptist State Convention, 1955), 1:529-530, 2:497, quoted in Murray, *Revival and Revivalism*, 315.

216 Roland Q. Leavell, "Evangelism," in *Encyclopedia of Southern Baptists*, ed. Clifton J. Allen (Nashville: Broadman, 1958), 415, quoted in Benjamin S. Tellinghuisen, "Developing the

> This viewpoint is incompatible with the facts of history.... Baptist churches were marked by aggressive evangelism long before the new era of the 1830s.... There is a great weight of evidence to sustain the assertion that definite Calvinistic beliefs did not inhibit evangelism among the Baptist churches before the 1830s.... It is not to be denied that hyper-Calvinism had some existence in the United States at the beginning of the nineteenth century but its features can be readily recognized and they were not those of any of the Baptist leaders.[217]

Despite evidence to the contrary, Finney's apparent success gave credit to his disparaging of Calvinism as a "theological" and "legal fiction" that "slanders God."[218]

This trend of conflating Calvinism with hyper-Calvinism is still alive and well today. For instance, the entry on "Hyper-Calvinism" in the 1992 *Encyclopedia of the Reformed Faith* concludes with the statement, "The description of hyper-Calvinism is, of course, made from within central or classic Calvinism/Reformed theology. *To people outside the Reformed faith it merely appears as a form of Calvinism*, no better or worse than others."[219]

Like those who came after him, the basis of Finney's agenda was to rewrite and reshape the history of revivalism. Pyke states,

> In this new theological climate, a climate which has largely prevailed in American evangelicalism to this day, the picture of Finney as a man embroiled in a lifelong controversy, *trying to justify his own radical measures and at the same time to stamp out a theological tradition which he hated, has been obscured.* The new views have prevailed, and Finney has emerged a great evangelist and revivalist folk hero.[220]

Pyke concludes that an "anti-theological bias" in the late nineteenth and into the twentieth century "was one of the factors behind the loss of an historically objective view of [Finney] by the next generation of Christians."[221]

The fact that many often mischaracterize John Gill and those that promote his works as hyper-Calvinistic helps to illuminate the tendency to conflate Calvinism with hyper-Calvinism. It is clear from the following and other statements in his writings that he was not a hyper-Calvinist:

New Baptist Catechism for Use at First Baptist Church of Farmington, Michigan" (PhD diss., Louisville, Southern Baptist Theological Seminary, 2021), 52, https://repository.sbts.edu/handle/10392/6511.

217 Murray, *Revival and Revivalism*, 315–17.

218 Finney, *Memoirs of Finney: Restored*, 58, 60; Finney, *Lectures on Revivals of Religion*, 197.

219 Peter Toon, "Hyper-Calvinism," in *Encyclopedia of the Reformed Faith*, ed. Donald K. McKim (Louisville: Westminster John Knox, 1992), 190 (emphasis added).

220 Pyke, "Finney and the Second Great Awakening," 34 (emphasis added).

221 Pyke, 57.

> It is true, the ministers of the gospel, though they ought not to offer and tender salvation to any, for which they have no commission, yet they may preach the gospel of salvation to all men, and declare, that *whosoever believes shall be saved;* for this they are commissioned to do ... But then this preaching of the gospel to all indefinitely, no ways contradicts the particular redemption and special salvation of the elect only; it being designed, and is blessed, for the effectual gathering of them to Christ; and does become *the power of God* to their *salvation,* and theirs only.[222]

Many who read his works fail to see the distinction he makes. According to Gill, the gospel is never *offered* or *proffered* to anyone. Something which is a fact established in eternity past that is carried out effectually in time to those for whom it was designed, the elect, cannot be proffered.

Peter Toon states that hyper-Calvinism is "a system of theology, or a system of the doctrines of God, man and grace, which was framed to exalt the honour and glory of God and did so at the expense of minimising the moral and spiritual responsibility of sinners to God."[223] He concludes that this leads to the notion that grace must only be offered to those for whom it was intended. This example is just one of many examples of the perpetuation of Finney's redefinition of Calvinism as hyper-Calvinism that persists today.

Effects of Revivalism

Many of the disastrous consequences of Finneyism were already felt in Charles H. Spurgeon's day, whose ministry overlapped somewhat with Finney's. In a sermon entitled "The Great Revival," preached on March 28, 1858, he shows the link between theology and methodology clearly:

> There are a number of revivals, which occur every now and then in our towns, and sometimes in our city, which I believe to be spurious and worthless. I have heard of people crowding in the morning, the afternoon, and the evening to hear some noted revivalist, and under his preaching some have screamed, have shrieked, have fallen down on the floor, have rolled themselves in convulsions, and afterwards, *when he has set a form for penitents, employing one or two decoy ducks to run out from the rest and make a confession of sin, hundreds have come forward,* impressed by that one sermon, and declared that they were, there and then, turned from the error of their ways.... All that I call a farce! There may be something good in it; but the outside looks to me to be so rotten, that I should scarcely trust myself to think that the good within comes to any very great amount. When people go to calculate so exactly by arithmetic, it always strikes me they have mistaken what

---

[222] John Gill, *The Cause of God and Truth,* A New Edition (1735–1738; repr., London: Thomas Tegg & Son, 1838), 303 (emphasis original).

[223] Peter Toon, *The Emergence of Hyper-Calvinism in English Nonconformity 1689–1765* (Wipf & Stock, 2011), 144.

> they are at.... The Holy Spirit, as the actual agent—the Word preached, and the prayers of the people, as the instruments—and we have thus explained the cause of a true revival of religion.[224]

Preaching on the revivalism of the late nineteenth century, Spurgeon lamented:

> Moreover, to stand up and cry, "Believe, believe, believe," without explaining what is to be believed, to lay the whole stress of salvation upon faith without explaining what salvation is, and showing that it means deliverance from the power as well as from the guilt of sin, may seem to a fervent revivalist to be the proper thing for the occasion, but those who have watched the result of such teaching have had grave cause to question whether as much hurt may not be done by it as good.[225]

Like many of his contemporaries, it is clear that Spurgeon had grave concerns about *revivalism* that was worked up through enthusiasm and human effort rather than as a supernatural event from God.

Effects on Baptist Theology and Methodology

Referring to the period around 1830, regarding the revivalism of Finney that was spreading throughout parts of the country, David Benedict writes, in a section of *Fifty Years Among the Baptists* entitled "On Religious Revivals in former Times":

> As far back as my recollection and researches extend, these seasons, for the most part, were like angel visits, few and far between.... During all this time scarcely any of the new measures of more modern times were adopted.... As a general thing, the old way of conducting meetings, whether in seasons of revivals or declensions, was pursued, and all attempts to produce a high state of feeling among the people were carefully avoided. Depth of feeling was the main thing desired by our most efficient men, whether in the pulpit or the conference room. They also made much dependence on the silent workings of the divine Spirit on the hearts of the people. On these agencies the Baptists made much more dependence than on multitudinous gatherings and bodily exercises. At length *protracted meetings* began to be much talked of far and near, and so many reports were circulated concerning the wonderful effects of them, that by many they were thought to be the very thing for promoting religious revivals.... In connection with these meetings came along a new sort of preachers, who went into the business of conducting them by new rules of their own. In the process of time

---

[224] C. H. Spurgeon, "The Great Revival," in *The New Park Street Pulpit Sermons*, vol. 4 (London: Passmore & Alabaster, 1858), 162, 164 (emphasis added).

[225] C. H. Spurgeon, "Faith and Regeneration," in *The Metropolitan Tabernacle Pulpit Sermons*, vol. 17 (London: Passmore & Alabaster, 1871), 133–34.

> the Baptists became a good deal engaged in these peculiar gatherings, and many of them seemed much pleased with them. The *revival ministers*, as they were called, soon became very popular.… But, in some cases, the old ministers and churches demurred, and were unwilling to have these new men, with their new notions, introduced among them … and … a new machinery in the working of conversion.… To see converts coming into a church by wholesale was a pleasing idea to many members … [b]ut another class of members had fearful forebodings for the future.[226]

Benedict is an example of one who saw the dangers of the methods used for conversion. Others spoke out, but those who favored the *new measures* soon drowned out their voices.

William McLoughlin claims that the Baptist Jacob Knapp "was almost as well known as Finney by 1840."[227] In his autobiography, Knapp approvingly states, "Shortly before I started as an evangelist, the Lord has raised up among the Presbyterians Charles G. Finney and Jedediah Burchard. And God, as we all know, has crowned the labors of these devoted men with marvellous success."[228] Knapp's autobiography clearly shows that Finney's methodology influenced him. Frank Grenville Beardsley states, "Elders Jacob Knapp and Jabez S. Swan were the pioneer evangelists of the [Baptist] denomination, and through their earnest efforts, greater attention was given to revivals, and the denomination entered upon a new era in the work of evangelization."[229] In his autobiography, Knapp writes, "Among Baptists, at the time when I started out, there was no one man who stood forth as the champion and exemplar of revival measures."[230]

He notes that his "new method of presenting the gospel captivated some and repelled others."[231] Murray states that Knapp's autobiography "proves that he was among the first of the Baptist practitioners of" the new measures and that he "came to regard his mission as the conversion of the Baptists to the new views."[232]

Knapp also went against the long-standing Baptist "traditions of having converts come before a committee, and wait a month before they could be baptized." He started the practice of instant baptism of converts "as fast as

---

226 Benedict, *Fifty Years Among the Baptists*, 200–203.

227 William G. McLoughlin, *Modern Revivalism: Charles Grandison Finney to Billy Graham* (1959; repr., Eugene, OR: Wipf & Stock, 2004), 140.

228 Jacob Knapp, *Autobiography of Elder Jacob Knapp* (New York: Sheldon, 1868), 40.

229 Frank Grenville Beardsley, *A History of American Revivals*, Third Edition (New York: American Tract Society, 1912), 164.

230 Knapp, *Autobiography of Elder Jacob Knapp*, 41.

231 Knapp, 68.

232 Murray, *Revival and Revivalism*, 312–13.

they found peace in believing with all their hearts."[233] He boasts in his autobiography, "Brother Everts and myself baptized ninety-six in one day."[234] Knapp was one of the pioneers of the Baptist emphasis on the number of conversions and baptisms. McLoughlin records that Knapp "claimed to have conducted 150 separate revivals and to have converted 100,000 persons by 1874, the year he died."[235] Knapp concludes, "[T]hose churches which did not sympathize with these new measures died out, and those ministers who opposed the progress of evangelical effort are forgotten, or are remembered only as men who misinterpreted the signs of the times."[236] As alluded, this was part of history's slow but gradual rewriting. Those whose influence finally won the day got to record the movement's history. Only a few forgotten sermons and letters in the dustbin of history remain of those who were unsuccessful in stemming the tide of revivalism.

History indicates that Jacob Knapp is the link between the theology and methodology of Finney and its encroachment into the Baptist denomination. In the preface to Knapp's autobiography, R. Jeffery states, "Posterity will speak of Elder Knapp as the pioneer and champion of modern evangelism."[237] Murray rightly notes that it "is an extraordinary claim, that it was the new men such as Knapp who introduced evangelism and 'revivals' among the Baptists in the 1830s and subsequently."[238] He contends that Beardsley, and others in later generations, accepted these claims as truth and "helped to teach subsequent generations to regard it as authentic history."[239] However, when Beardsley stated that "Baptists shared … to no inconsiderable extent in the Awakenings of 1800," he inadvertently demonstrated that revivals were not actually *introduced* to the Baptists by Knapp.[240]

Nevertheless, Beardsley perpetuates the polemic regarding the poor condition of some churches. He states they "did not favor special efforts to promote revivals of religion." Thus, they were "tinctured with the hyper-Calvinism of the period, which looked askance upon all human attempts to

233 Knapp, *Autobiography of Elder Jacob Knapp*, 108.

234 Knapp, 108.

235 McLoughlin, *Modern Revivalism*, 140.

236 Knapp, *Autobiography of Elder Jacob Knapp*, 47.

237 R. Jeffery, preface to *Autobiography of Elder Jacob Knapp*, by Jacob Knapp (New York: Sheldon, 1868), iv.

238 Murray, *Revival and Revivalism*, 314.

239 Murray, 314.

240 Beardsley, *A History of American Revivals*, 163.

effect the regeneration of men."[241] Similarly, McLoughlin perpetuated the idea of Finney, ridiculing those who deemed God sovereign over salvation.

Patrick McIntyre's book *The Graham Formula: Why most Decisions for Christ are Ineffective* does not go far enough in its analysis of the effects of Revivalism and Finney's new measures. McIntyre recounts the story of a woman who was "careful never to lead someone to the conclusion they were saved unless they bore obvious fruit." She was assisting as a counselor at a Franklin Graham crusade. After Graham led a large group of people in the "usual salvation prayer," she "hoped that many were led of the Holy Spirit when they prayed." Then she was horrified when Franklin Graham said, "If you prayed that prayer and meant it, God has just forgiven you. He just washed the slate clean … this is your spiritual birthday." Many would rightly be horrified if they heard someone proclaim this. However, it is what the author recounts next that is most troubling. He writes, "It was then she remembered the follow-up system. She thanked God that BGEA insisted counselors call inquirers within forty-eight hours of the crusade, church ministers visit the homes and each inquirer enroll in a Bible study course, giving them every opportunity to be saved."[242] It appears that McIntyre is indicating approval of the idea that it is OK to tell people that salvation has occurred the moment they pray the prayer, as long as someone follows up with an opportunity for them actually to be saved at some point soon. This deceptive method does not accord with Scripture. It inevitably leads to numerous false converts. May will go through life assured that they were born again that day. They will assume that since Franklin Graham told them they were saved, there is no need to worry about their salvation. Thus they will go on living the same unchanged life they always have. This fact is just one of the many rotten fruits produced by Finney's methodology, based on faulty theology.

Effects on the Understanding of God and His Role in Conversion

Pink's classic, *The Sovereignty of God,* was initially published in 1918, in the aftermath of Revivalism. Finney and those who follow in his footsteps, whether intentionally or not, deny the sovereignty of God. Pink summarizes the effects of this theology:

> To say that God the Father has purposed the salvation of all mankind, that God the Son died with the express intention of saving the whole human race, and that God the Holy Spirit is now seeking to win the world to Christ; when, as a matter of common observation, it is apparent that the great majority of our fellowmen

---

241 Beardsley, 163.

242 Patrick McIntyre, *The Graham Formula: Why Most Decisions for Christ Are Ineffective* (Mammoth Spring, AR: White Harvest, 2005), 31–32.

> are dying in sin, and passing into a hopeless eternity; is to say that God the Father is *disappointed,* that God the Son is *dissatisfied,* and that God the Holy Spirit is *defeated.* We have stated the issue baldly, but there is no escaping the conclusion. To argue that God is "trying His best" to save all mankind, but that the majority of men will not let Him save them, is to insist that the will of the Creator is impotent, and that the will of the creature is omnipotent.[243]

Unfortunately, this is the *other gospel* preached in many churches today. It is a form of moral change based on one's *decision* to *invite Christ into their heart.* The biblical truth is that conversion results from the omnipotent God of the universe changing one's wicked and rebellious heart so that it now wants God. Thus, one lives a transformed life, as the result of that change, in gratitude to the One that graciously condescended to save such a wretched sinner.

Effects on Views of What Church Membership Constitutes

Albert B. Dod brings out an enormous implication of Finney's system. He shows that Finney intends to speedily admit a person to church membership once that person makes an *immediate* profession, upon excitement by the new measures. Dod caricatures Finney's supposed response to questioning new converts before admission to membership. He writes, "Hold, hold, cries Mr. Finney, take care how you ensnare the conscience of this young convert by examining him too extensively or minutely on doctrinal points."[244] Once Finney has thus ensured his professors' open entrance into the church, Dod asks:

> But how shall they be kept there? … [T]hey shall be kept in ignorance of the standards of the church they have entered. Young converts, he says, ought to be indoctrinated, but he avowedly excludes from the means of indoctrination, "teaching the catechism." This would answer if he could only keep in the first ones until he had introduced a majority into every church who should know nothing of the catechism or confession of faith.[245]

Sadly, this has happened in many Baptist churches in subsequent generations. They began to accept measures to *bring about* conversions and *revival.* The focus shifted from doctrinal purity to tallying the numbers of converts. Consequently, many churches did just as Finney had intended and became vehemently opposed to confessions of faith and catechisms. Catechizing, which had been a bulwark for maintaining sound doctrine

---

[243] Pink, *The Sovereignty of God*, 26 (emphasis original).

[244] Dod, "On Revivals of Religion," 650.

[245] Dod, 650.

among Baptists at the founding of the Southern Baptist Convention, was largely abandoned. This anti-confessional and anti-catechism stance is still predominant in most Baptist churches.

One of the results of these methodologies is numerous false converts. They believe salvation has occurred but continue to live as if nothing has changed. In fact, nothing has changed; they were never truly born again. Scripture is clear that "unless one is born again he cannot see the kingdom of God" (John 3:3).

Summary

Phillip R. Johnson, in an article entitled "A Wolf in Sheep's Clothing: How Charles Finney's Theology Ravaged the Evangelical Movement," summarizes the devastating fallout of Finney's doctrines:

> Charles Grandison Finney was a heretic.... The arguments he employed to sustain [his] views were nearly always rationalistic and philosophical, not biblical. To canonize this man as an evangelical hero is to ignore the facts of what he stood for.... By no stretch of the imagination does Finney deserve to be regarded as an evangelical. By corrupting the doctrine of justification by faith; by denying the doctrines of original sin and total depravity, by minimizing the sovereignty of God while enthroning the power of the human will; and above all, by undermining the doctrine of substitutionary atonement, *Finney filled the bloodstream of American evangelicalism with poisons that have kept the movement maimed even to this day.*[246]

Monte E. Wilson states, "Finneyism, in seeking to close the sale, actually served to close hearts and minds to the biblical message of Salvation, leaving people deceived as to their spiritual state, wondering why the Christian life eluded them."[247] The result of a theology of *decisionism* is numerous false converts who try to live a Christian life when they have never been regenerated and indwelt with the Holy Spirit. The Holy Spirit is the only power that enables one to do what God commands.

Unfortunately, the aftermath of this new theology and its associated measures linger in evangelicalism today. In many instances, the focus is on numbers rather than true converts, which directly reflects one's view of conversion. Suppose conversion is a decision on man's part rather than a sovereign act of God, who "will have mercy on whom [he will] have mercy" (Romans 9:15). In that case, one has grounds to boast, contrary to Ephesians

---

246 Phillip R. Johnson, "A Wolf in Sheep's Clothing: How Charles Finney's Theology Ravaged the Evangelical Movement," 1999, http://www.romans45.org/articles/finney.htm.

247 Monte E. Wilson, "Charles Grandison Finney: The Aftermath," *Reformation and Revival* 6, no. 1 (1997): 6, https://www.galaxie.com/article/rar006-1-005.

2:9. Then the focus will be on the results rather than preaching the gospel and allowing the wind of the Holy Spirit to blow where he wills (John 3:8).

7

CONCLUSION

Much of modern evangelicalism must remove the rose-colored glasses of the whitewashed versions and treatments of Finney's works and look at what he wrote and taught. In doing so, hopefully, it will become evident that Finney's teaching is heretical. One can then see that Finney's theology is directly to blame for much of the theological drift and aberration in Baptists and the evangelical church at large.

Summary of the Effects of Finney's Theology and Methodology

Robert Pyke, writing in 1997, aptly summarizes the devastating aftermath of Finney:

> Though he lived just in the last century, was eminently famous, and left voluminous writings, the historical Finney can be difficult to recover. This circumstance probably has several causes. *One is the triumph of Arminian theology in American religion. Finney is the key figure in the great theological shift which took place in America in the nineteenth century.* The theology of conversion was no longer theocentric, the focus in evangelism now being on man and his responsibility, not on God, His holiness, and His saving mercy. Arminianism's man-centered theology had obscured much of the church's heritage.[248]

In 1835, Albert B. Dod stated, "It is now generally understood that the numerous converts of the new measures have been, in most cases, like the morning cloud and the early dew. In some places, not a half, a fifth, or even a tenth part of them remain."[249] Pyke similarly concludes that what "soon became apparent with Finney's revivals was that great numbers of the

---

[248] Pyke, "Finney and the Second Great Awakening," 33–34 (emphasis added).

[249] Dod, "On Revivals of Religion," 660.

converts were spurious … [and] the long-term results were often devastating."[250]

Most who follow in Finney's footsteps do not go as far as he did and embrace Pelagianism. Yet, the man-centered Arminian theology that resulted from the popularization of his theology and methodology is still rampant in the church today. Pyke aptly concludes, "Finney … spent his life … in one long, concerted battle against Calvinistic orthodoxy … [in which] an evangelical sea-change occurred, and *Arminianism has been the dominant impulse in American evangelicalism since Finney's time.*"[251] "Widely regarded as the father of modern revivalism, *Finney represents the watershed in the shift from Calvinism to Arminianism as the dominant theology.…* Finney's legacy shaped the theology and methodology of evangelism generally, *and Southern Baptist evangelism particularly,*" surmises Rick Nelson.[252]

While Finney was Pelagian in his theology, the lasting influence of his theology and methodology on Baptists was a theological shift from their Calvinistic roots to Arminianism as the dominant theology. Logically this entailed the subsequent changes in methods that occur when one's thinking changes from a God-centered approach to a man-centric one.

Practical and Pastoral Application for the Church Today

One should carefully evaluate how they respond to the drift in Baptist theology. One would do well to heed the words of Iain Murray in his Prefatory Note to "A Letter to the Rev. Mr. John Wesley." Whitefield wrote the letter in response to Wesley's publication of a sermon entitled "Free Grace," which was a direct attack on the doctrine of election:

> [W]hile their public co-operation was thus seriously disturbed, *his personal affection for the Wesleys as Christians was preserved to the last.* In this respect Whitfield teaches us a needful lesson. *Doctrinal differences between believers should never lead to personal antagonism.* Error must be opposed even when held by fellow members of Christ, but if that opposition cannot co-exist with a true love for all saints and a longing for their spiritual prosperity then it does not glorify God nor promote the edification of the Church.[253]

The preface to Baptist minister John Williams's (1747–1795) work defending believer's baptism shows his spirit toward all believers. He

---

[250] Pyke, "Finney and the Second Great Awakening," 42.

[251] Pyke, 58 (emphasis added).

[252] Rick Nelson, "How Does Doctrine Affect Evangelism? The Divergent Paths of Asahel Nettleton and Charles Finney," *The Founder's Journal*, no. 33 (Summer 1998): 1, http://www.gracesermons.com/hisbygrace/doctrine.html (emphasis added).

[253] Whitefield, *George Whitefield's Journals*, 568 (emphasis added).

cordially but valiantly contended for the truths that Scripture convinced him of. He writes:

> I am not overbearing on others, or bigoted to those of my principles which are not essential to salvation. I have universally endevoured to promote a catholic spirit, with peace and concord, in the Israel of God. But, nevertheless, I am set for the defence of the Gospel; and, as such, circumstances often occur, that require me to contend for the faith and order of Christ's Church.[254]

Richard Baxter, in a section on the necessity of union and communion among ministers, shows a similar spirit that is worthy of emulation when dealing with those who hold false doctrine:

> Ministers must smart when the church is wounded, and being so far from being the leaders in divisions, that they should take it as a principal part of their work to prevent and heal them.... The Scripture-sufficiency must be maintained, and nothing beyond it imposed on others; and if Papists, or others, call to us for the standard and rule of our religion, it is the Bible that we must shew them, rather than any Confessions of Churches, or writings of men. We must learn to difference well between certainties and uncertainties, necessaries and unnecessaries, catholic verities ... and private opinions; and to lay the stress of the church's peace upon the former, and not upon the latter.... And we must learn to see the true state of Controversies, and reduce them to the very point where the difference lieth, and not to make them seem greater than they are. Instead of quarrelling with our brethren, we must combine against the common adversaries; Ministers must associate, and hold communion, and correspondence, and constant meetings to those ends; and smaller differences of judgment are not to interrupt them. [255]

The Rev. Daniel Sharp, D. D., in a sketch of William Staughton, D. D., Baptist minister from 1793–1829, highlights Staughton's "catholicity of spirit" by quoting from his message at the dedication of a new meeting house of another denomination:

> I know I am but adding a voice to the thoughts of my brother through whose ministrations this house has been raised, and of the members of the Church in general, when I give a cordial welcome to every preacher of Jesus to assist in its holy services. The points in which we differ from our Christian brethren of other denominations, compared with those in which we all agree, bear no greater proportion to each other, than does the trembling lustre of a star to the meridian blaze of the summer sun. When Christian ingenuousness proceeds to state

---

[254] Sprague, *Annals of the American Pulpit*, VI:132.

[255] Richard Baxter, "The Reformed Pastor," in *The Practical Works of the Rev. Richard Baxter*, vol. 14 (London: James Duncan, 1830), 131–32.

religious sentiment with plainness and simplicity, Christian love looks anxiously for the moment when bigotry shall expire with the flames it has kindled.[256]

One should strive for the same spirit as these men of years past. They "earnestly contend[ed] for the truth once and for all delivered to the saints" (Jude 3) when necessary while not being dogmatic about *disputed* things on which Scripture is not clear. One can love and fellowship with brothers and sisters from other denominations and theological traditions that hold the fundamentals of the gospel while disagreeing with them on disputed or secondary things. However, one should never allow the thought of unity to cause us to waver in our opinion on things central to the Christian faith. As stated in the introduction, Arminians and Calvinists can debate these issues and agree to disagree on many of them as fellow Christians and brothers in Christ. Still, both should reject those who, like Finney, hold Pelagian views that make God impotent and man omnipotent. We must always remain *valiant for truth,* like the character from Bunyan's allegory.[257]

Concluding Admonition

The title of Karl Dahlfred's book, *Theology Drives Methodology*, is an apt description of the essence of our problem.[258] May Christians seek to remove the rose-colored glasses from the legacy of Finney so that they can see the situation as it truly was and is. Until churches return to a biblical theology of conversion, they will continue to use methodologies that place man's will above God's sovereignty in salvation. Only then can the church be continually reforming its practice and theology according to the Word of God, not man's word and methods.

---

[256] Sprague, *Annals of the American Pulpit*, VI:342.

[257] John Bunyan, *The Pilgrim's Progress* (1678; repr., Bellingham, WA: Logos Bible Software, 2006).

[258] Dahlfred, *Theology Drives Methodology.*

BIBLIOGRAPHY

"A Glossary of Terms." *Christian History Magazine*, no. 20: Charles Finney: American Revivalism (1988): 24–26. https://christianhistoryinstitute.org/uploaded/50cf76f3653009.10451180.pdf.

Alexander, Archibald. "An Inquiry into That Inability Under Which the Sinner Labours, and Whether It Furnishes Any Excuse for His Neglect of Duty." *The Biblical Repertory and Theological Review*, New Series, III, no. 1–4 (1831).

———. "The Doctrine of Original Sin as Held by the Church, Both before and after the Reformation." *The Biblical Repertory and Theological Review*, New Series, 2, no. 1–4 (1830).

———. "The Early History of Pelagianism." *The Biblical Repertory and Theological Review*, New Series, 2, no. 1–4 (1830).

Alexander, James Waddel. *Forty Years' Familiar Letters of James W. Alexander, D. D.: Constituting, with Notes, a Memoir of His Life*. Edited by John Hall. Vol. 2. New York: Charles Scribner, 1860.

———. "The Holy Flock." In *The New York Pulpit in the Revival of 1858: A Memorial Volume of Sermons*, 13–37. New York: Sheldon, Blakeman, 1858.

Armitage, Thomas. *A History of the Baptists: Traced by Their Vital Principles and Practices, from the Time of Our Lord and Saviour Jesus Christ to the Present.* Revised and Enlarged Edition. New York: Bryan, Taylor, 1890.

Asbury, Francis. *The Journal and Letters of Francis Asbury*. Edited by J. Manning Potts. Vol. III. London: Epworth, 1958.

Ascol, Thomas K. *From the Protestant Reformation to the Southern Baptist Convention: What Hath Geneva to Do with Nashville*. Revised edition. Cape Coral, FL: Founders, 2013.

———. *"Traditional" Theology & the SBC: An Interaction with, and Response to, The Traditional Statement of God's Plan of Salvation.* Revised Edition. Cape Coral, FL: Founders, 2018.

Barry, John D., David Bomar, Derek R. Brown, Rachel Klippenstein, Douglas Mangum, Carrie Sinclair Wolcott, Lazarus Wentz, Elliot Ritzema, and Wendy Widder, eds. "Pelagianism." In *The Lexham Bible Dictionary*. Bellingham, WA: Lexham Press, 2016.

Baxter, Richard. "The Reformed Pastor." In *The Practical Works of the Rev. Richard Baxter*, Vol. 14. London: James Duncan, 1830.

Beardsley, Frank Grenville. *A History of American Revivals*. Third Edition. New York: American Tract Society, 1912.

Belyea, Gordon L. "Origins of the Particular Baptists." *Themelios* 32, no. 3 (April 2007): 40–67. http://tgc-documents.s3.amazonaws.com/themelios/Themelios32.3.pdf.

Benedict, David. *A General History of the Baptist Denomination in America: And Other Parts of the World.* Vol. 2. Boston: Manning & Loring, 1813.

———. *Fifty Years Among the Baptists*. 1860. Reprint, Paris, AR: Baptist Standard Bearer, 2001.

Boyce, James Petigru. *Abstract of Systematic Theology*. 1887. Reprint, Bellingham, WA: Logos Bible Software, 2010.

Bunyan, John. *The Pilgrim's Progress*. 1678. Reprint, Bellingham, WA: Logos Bible Software, 2006.

Caldwell, Robert W., III. *Theologies of the American Revivalists: From Whitefield to Finney*. Downers Grove, IL: InterVarsity Press, 2017.

Carroll, B. H. *The Pastoral Epistles of Paul, 1 and 2 Peter, Jude, and 1, 2, and 3 John*. Edited by J. B. Cranfill. New and Complete Edition. Vol. XVI. An Interpretation of the English Bible. Nashville: Broadman, 1947.

Chemnitz, Martin. *Examination of the Council of Trent.* Translated by Fred Kramer. Electronic ed. Vol. 1. St. Louis: Concordia, 1999.

Cook, Matthew W. "The Impact of Revivalism upon Baptist Faith and Practice in the American South Prior to the Civil War." PhD diss., Baylor University, 2009. https://baylor-ir.tdl.org/bitstream/handle/2104/5372/Matthew_Cook_phd.pdf.

Criswell, W. A. "Doctrine of Predestination." Sermon, First Baptist Church of Dallas, November 20, 1955. https://wacriswell.com/sermons/1955/doctrine-of-predestination/.

———. "The Effectual Calling of God." Sermon, First Baptist Church of Dallas, June 5, 1983. https://wacriswell.com/sermons/1983/the-effectual-calling-of-god/.

Dagg, J. L. *Manual of Theology, First Part: A Treatise on Christian Doctrine.* Charleston, SC: Southern Baptist Publication Society, 1859.

Dahlfred, Karl. *Theology Drives Methodology: Conversion in the Theology of Charles Finney and John Nevin.* Monee, IL: Createspace, 2012.

D'Aubigné, J. H. Merle. *History of the Reformation in the Sixteenth Century.* Translated by Henry Beveridge. Vol. 5. Glasgow: William Collins, 1862.

Dickinson, Jonathan. "The Nature and Necessity of Regeneration." In *Salvation in Full Color: Twenty Sermons by Great Awakening Preachers*, edited by Richard Owen Roberts, 135–54. 1743. Reprint, Wheaton, IL: International Awakening, 1994.

Dod, Albert B. "Lectures on Revivals of Religion and Sermons on Various Subjects." *The Biblical Repertory and Theological Review*, New Series, 7, no. 1–4 (1835).

Edwards, Jonathan. "A Faithful Narrative of the Surprising Work of God, in the Conversion of Many Hundred Souls, in Northampton, and the Neighboring Towns and Villages of New Hampshire, in New England; in a Letter to the Rev. Dr. Colman, of Boston." In *The Works of Jonathan Edwards*, edited by Edward Hickman, 1:344–64. 1834. Reprint, Edinburgh: Banner of Truth Trust, 1974.

Fairchild, J. H. "Glossary." In *Finney's Systematic Theology*, Abridged. 1846–1847. Reprint, Minneapolis: Bethany Fellowship, 1976.

Feldmeth, Nathan P. "SemiPelagianism." In *Pocket Dictionary of Church History: Over 300 Terms Clearly and Concisely Defined.* Downers Grove: InterVarsity Press, 2008.

Finney, Charles G. "Doctrine of Election." In *Sermons on Important Subjects*, 209–20. New York: John S. Taylor, 1836.

———. *Finney's Systematic Theology.* Edited by J. H. Fairchild. Abridged. 1846–1847. Reprint, Minneapolis: Bethany Fellowship, 1976.

———. "Justification by Faith." In *Lectures to Professing Christians*, 210–27. New York: John S. Taylor, 1837.

———. *Lectures on Revivals of Religion.* New York: Fleming H. Revell, 1888.

———. *Lectures on Systematic Theology: Embracing Ability (Natural, Moral and Gracious) Repentance, Impenitence, Faith and Unbelief.* Vol. 2. Oberlin, OH: Fitch, 1847.

———. *Lectures on Systematic Theology: Embracing Lectures on Moral Government, Together with Atonement, Moral and Physical Depravity, Regeneration, Philosophical Theories, and Evidences of Regeneration.* Vol. 1. Oberlin, OH: Fitch, 1846.

———. "Sinners Bound to Change Their Own Hearts." In *Sermons on Important Subjects*, 3–42. New York: John S. Taylor, 1836.

———. *The Memoirs of Charles G. Finney: The Complete Restored Text.* Edited by Garth M. Rosell and Richard A. G. Dupuis. Grand Rapids: Zondervan, 1997.

———. "Total Depravity." In *Sermons on Important Subjects*, 113–40. New York: John S. Taylor, 1836.

———. "Traditions of the Elders." In *Sermons on Important Subjects*, 67–90. New York: John S. Taylor, 1836.

Forrester, Duncan B. "Carey, William (1761–1834)." In *Encyclopedia of the Reformed Faith*, edited by Donald K. McKim, 58. Louisville: Westminster John Knox, 1992.

Foster, Frank Hugh. *A Genetic History of the New England Theology.* Chicago: University of Chicago Press, 1907.

Gamble, Richard C. "Socinianism." In *Encyclopedia of the Reformed Faith*, edited by Donald K. McKim, 355. Louisville: Westminster John Knox, 1992.

George, Timothy. *Baptist Confessions, Covenants, and Catechisms.* Nashville: Broadman & Holman, 1996.

Gill, John. *An Exposition of the New Testament.* 3 vols. 1763. Reprint, London: Mathews & Leigh, 1809.

———. *The Cause of God and Truth.* A New Edition. 1735–1738. Reprint, London: Thomas Tegg & Son, 1838.

Godfrey, W. Robert. *Saving the Reformation: The Pastoral Theology of the Canons of Dort.* Orlando, FL: Reformation Trust, 2019.

Grenz, Stanley, David Guretzki, and Cherith Fee Nordling. "Augustine, Augustinianism (354–430)." In *Pocket Dictionary of Theological Terms.* Downers Grove: InterVarsity Press, 1999.

Haykin, Michael A.G. Foreword to *Confessing the Faith: The 1689 Baptist Confession for the 21st Century*, 5–6. Cape Coral, FL: Founders Press, 2012.

Henry, Matthew. *Matthew Henry's Commentary on the Whole Bible: Complete and Unabridged in One Volume.* 1706. Reprint, Peabody: Hendrickson, 1994.

Hill, John L. Foreword to *The Pastoral Epistles of Paul, 1 and 2 Peter, Jude, and 1, 2, and 3 John*, by B. H. Carroll, v–vi. edited by J. B. Cranfill, New and Complete Edition. An Interpretation of the English Bible. Nashville: Broadman, 1947.

Hodge, Charles. "The New Divinity Tried. Review of 'the New Divinity Tried;' or, an Examination of the Rev. Mr. Rand's Strictures on a Sermon Delivered by the Rev. C. J. Finney, on Making a New Heart by C. J. Finney." *The Biblical Repertory and Theological Review* IV, no. 1–4 (1832).

Horton, Michael S. "The Legacy of Charles Finney." *Modern Reformation* 4, no. 1 (February 1995): 5–9. https://modernreformation.org/resource-library/articles/the-legacy-of-charles-finney/.

Hovey, Alvah. *A Memoir of the Life and Times of the Rev. Isaac Backus, A.M.* Boston: Gould & Lincoln, 1859.

Jeffery, R. Preface to *Autobiography of Elder Jacob Knapp*, by Jacob Knapp, iii–iv. New York: Sheldon, 1868.

Johnson, Phillip R. "A Wolf in Sheep's Clothing: How Charles Finney's Theology Ravaged the Evangelical Movement," 1999. http://www.romans45.org/articles/finney.htm.

Kendall, Robert Tillman. "The Rise and Demise of Calvinism in the Southern Baptist Convention." MA thesis, University of Louisville, 1973. https://www.proquest.com/openview/257efa04cdc28990898524657353276c.

Kennedy, Earl Wm. "Taylor, Nathaniel William (1786–1858)." In *Encyclopedia of the Reformed Faith*, edited by Donald K. McKim, 361.

Louisville, KY: Westminster John Knox, 1992.

Kerfoot, F. H. "What We Believe According to the Scriptures." In *The Doctrines of Our Faith: A Convenient Handbook for Use in Normal Classes, Sacred Literature Courses and Individual Study*, by Edwin Charles Dargan. Nashville: Sunday School Board, 1905.

Knapp, Jacob. *Autobiography of Elder Jacob Knapp*. New York: Sheldon, 1868.

Lawrence, Michael. *Conversion: How God Creates a People*. 9Marks: Building Healthy Churches. Wheaton, IL: Crossway, 2017.

Lemke, Steve W. "History or Revisionist History? How Calvinistic Were the Overwhelming Majority of Baptists and Their Confessions in the South until the Twentieth Century?" *Southwestern Journal of Theology* 57, no. 2 (Spring 2015): 227–54. https://swbtsv7.s3.amazonaws.com/media/Theology_Journal/57.2/57.2_Lemke.pdf.

Lloyd-Jones, David Martyn. "Living the Christian Life." In *The Puritans: Their Origins and Successors: Addresses Delivered at the Puritan and Westminster Conferences 1959–1978*, 303–25. Edinburgh: Banner of Truth Trust, 2016.

———. "Revival: An Historical and Theological Survey." In *The Puritans: Their Origins and Successors: Addresses Delivered at the Puritan and Westminster Conferences 1959–1978*, 1–23. Edinburg: Banner of Truth Trust, 2016.

Long, Arthur J. "Unitarianism." In *The Dictionary of Historical Theology*, edited by Trevor A. Hart, 557–59. Carlisle, Cumbria, U.K.: Paternoster, 2000.

Lumpkin, William Latane. *Baptist Confessions of Faith*. Valley Forge, PA: Judson, 1959.

Luther, Martin. *Martin Luther on the Bondage of the Will; to the Venerable Mister Erasmus of Rotterdam, 1525*. Translated by Edward Thomas Vaughan. London: T. Hamilton, 1823.

McBeth, H. Leon. *The Baptist Heritage*. Nashville: Broadman & Holman, 1987.

McIntyre, Patrick. *The Graham Formula: Why Most Decisions for Christ Are Ineffective*. Mammoth Spring, AR: White Harvest, 2005.

McLoughlin, William G. *Modern Revivalism: Charles Grandison Finney to Billy Graham*. 1959. Reprint, Eugene, OR: Wipf & Stock, 2004.

Mell, P. H., Jr. *Life of Patrick Hues Mell*. Louisville: Baptist Book Concern,

1895.

Mell, Patrick Hues. *Predestination and the Saints' Perseverance: Stated and Defended from the Objections of Arminians, in a Review of Two Sermons*. Charleston, SC: Southern Baptist Publication Society, 1851.

Murray, Iain H. *Revival and Revivalism: The Making and Marring of American Evangelicalism; 1750 – 1858*. Edinburgh: Banner of Truth Trust, 2017.

Nelson, Rick. "How Does Doctrine Affect Evangelism? The Divergent Paths of Asahel Nettleton and Charles Finney." *The Founder's Journal*, no. 33 (Summer 1998). http://www.gracesermons.com/hisbygrace/doctrine.html.

Nettles, Thomas J. Afterword to *"Traditional" Theology & the SBC: An Interaction with, and Response to, The Traditional Statement of God's Plan of Salvation*, Revised Edition., 88–92. Cape Coral, FL: Founders, 2018.

———. *By His Grace and for His Glory: A Historical, Theological and Practical Study of the Doctrines of Grace in Baptist Life*. Revised and Expanded 20th Anniversary Edition. Cape Coral, FL: Founders, 2006.

———. *Living by Revealed Truth: The Life and Pastoral Theology of Charles Haddon Spurgeon*. Fearn, Ross-Shire: Mentor, 2015.

Nettles, Thomas J., and Steve Weaver. *Teaching Truth, Training Hearts: The Study of Catechisms in Baptist Life*. Revised edition. Cape Coral, FL: Founders, 2017.

Packer, J. I. *Concise Theology: A Guide to Historic Christian Beliefs*. Wheaton, IL: Tyndale House, 1993.

Pink, Arthur W. *The Sovereignty of God.* Fourth Edition. Swengel, PA: Bible Truth Depot, 1949.

Porter, Ebenezer. *Letters on the Religious Revivals Which Prevailed about the Beginning of the Present Century*. Boston: Congregational Board, 1858.

Pyke, Robert. "Charles G. Finney and the Second Great Awakening." *Reformation and Revival* 6, no. 1 (1997): 33–60. https://www.galaxie.com/article/rar06-1-03.

Ryland, John C. *The Beauty of Social Religion, or, the Nature and Glory of a Gospel Church, Represented in a Circular Letter.* Northamptonshire Baptist Association. Northampton: T. Dicey, 1777.

Semple, Robert Baylor. *A History of the Rise and Progress of the Baptists in Virginia*. Richmond: Published by the Author, John O'Lynch, Printer, 1810.

Smith, Jay E. "The Theology Of Charles Finney: A System Of Self-Reformation." *Trinity Journal* 13, no. 1 (1992): 61–93. https://www.galaxie.com/article/trinj013-1-004.

Southern Baptist Convention. "Comparison Chart – The Baptist Faith and Message." sbc.net. Accessed December 18, 2021. https://bfm.sbc.net/comparison-chart/.

Spilsbery, John. *A Treatise Concerning the Lawfull Subject of Baptism*. Second Edition Corrected and Enlarged. London: Henry Hills, 1652.

Sprague, William B. *Annals of the American Pulpit, or, Commemorative Notices of Distinguished American Clergymen of Various Denominations: From the Early Settlement of the Country to the Close of the Year Eighteen Hundred and Fifty-Five: With Historical Introductions*. Vol. VI. New York: R. Carter, 1860.

Spring, Gardiner. *Personal Reminiscences of the Life and Times of Gardiner Spring, Pastor of the Brick Presbyterian Church, in the City of New York*. Vol. 1. 2 vols. New York: Charles Scribner, 1866.

Sproul, R. C. *The Holiness of God*. Wheaton, IL: Tyndale House, 2013.

Spurgeon, C. H. "Christ Crucified." In *The New Park Street Pulpit Sermons*, 1:49–60. London: Passmore & Alabaster, 1855.

———. "Faith and Regeneration." In *The Metropolitan Tabernacle Pulpit Sermons*, 17:133–44. London: Passmore & Alabaster, 1871.

———. "The Great Revival." In *The New Park Street Pulpit Sermons*, 4:161–68. London: Passmore & Alabaster, 1858.

Tellinghuisen, Benjamin S. "Developing the New Baptist Catechism for Use at First Baptist Church of Farmington, Michigan." PhD diss., Southern Baptist Theological Seminary, 2021. https://repository.sbts.edu/handle/10392/6511.

Toon, Peter. "Hyper-Calvinism." In *Encyclopedia of the Reformed Faith*, edited by Donald K. McKim, 190. Louisville: Westminster John Knox, 1992.

———. *The Emergence of Hyper-Calvinism in English Nonconformity 1689–1765*. Wipf & Stock, 2011.

Tyler, Bennet. *Nettleton and His Labours: Being the Memoir of Dr. Nettleton.* Edinburgh: T&T Clark, 1854.

Warfield, Benjamin Breckinridge. "Oberlin Perfectionism." *The Princeton Theological Review* XIX, no. 1–4 (1921).

Whitefield, George. *George Whitefield's Journals.* Edited by Iain Murray. Edinburgh: Banner of Truth Trust, 1989.

———. "Letter CCCCLVIII." In *The Works of the Reverend George Whitefield,* 1:442. London: Edward & Charles Dilly, 1871.

Wilson, Monte E. "Charles Grandison Finney: The Aftermath." *Reformation and Revival* 6, no. 1 (1997): 95–101. https://www.galaxie.com/article/rar006-1-005.

Witherspoon, John. *The Works of the Rev. John Witherspoon.* Philadelphia: William W. Woodward, 1801.

ABOUT THE AUTHOR

David C. Hacker (DVM, Louisiana State University; BTh, MTh, DTh, International Christian College and Seminary) is currently enrolled in the MDiv program at Grace Bible Theological Seminary, Conway, AR, and is an avid studier of church history.

www.ingramcontent.com/pod-product-compliance
Ingram Content Group UK Ltd.
Pitfield, Milton Keynes, MK11 3LW, UK
UKHW041850190726
13854UKWH00002B/817